From Likes To Profits

A Guide to Choosing the Most Profitable Social Media Platforms for Your Brand

VERONICA GOLDSPIEL

Copyright © 2024 Veronica Goldspiel

All rights reserved.

All rights reserved. No part of this publication may be reproduced, distributed, or transmitted in any form or by any means, including photocopying, recording, or other electronic or mechanical methods, or by any information storage and retrieval system without prior written permission of the publisher, except in the case of very brief quotations embodied in critical reviews and certain other noncommercial uses permitted by copyright law.

This book is designed to provide accurate and authoritative information in regard to the subject matter herein. It is sold with the understanding that the author and publisher is not engaged in rendering legal, accounting, or other professional services. If you require legal advice or other expert assistance, you should seek the services of a competent professional.

While the author has made every effort to provide accurate website addresses and other information at the time of publication, neither the publisher nor the author assumes any responsibility for errors or changes that occur after publication. Further, the publisher does not have any control over and does not assume any responsibility for author or third-party websites or their content.

ISBN: 979-8-9903604-0-2

DEDICATION

This book is dedicated to my husband, Alan, for always being an inspiration to me! I am so lucky to have you by my side! Love you!

CONTENTS

	Acknowledgments	i
	INTRODUCTION	1
1	Why Your Organization Needs a Social Media Presence	10
2	Top 3 Must-Haves for Every Business	21
3	Who's Your Ideal Client or Customer?	38
4	X (Formerly Known as Twitter)	59
5	Instagram	65
6	Pinterest	71
7	LinkedIn	76
8	YouTube	81
9	Snapchat	88
10	Facebook	92
11	Keep It Simple and Have Fun	100
	FINAL WORDS	107
	ABOUT THE AUTHOR	124
	OTHER BOOKS BY AUTHOR	126

FREE GIFT FOR MY READERS

I have some special gifts for my readers! Below are some free gifts to help your business or brand advance "From Likes to Profits".

Your **FREE** gifts include:

- ❖ **2024 Easy Reference Social Media Demographics Chart** - A great reference to remind you of the different social media platforms and their specific demographics.
- ❖ **Discovering Your Ideal Customers or Clients Worksheet** – Gain clarity on your ideal customer avatar by analyzing demographics, interests, and identifying common traits.
- ❖ **Top 10 Things to Consider BEFORE Hiring a Social Media Manager** – Evaluate your business needs and objectives to determine the specific skills and expertise required from a social media manager.
- ❖ **PRIVATE FACEBOOK GROUP** – *Small Business Wealth Marketing Group*: Get your questions answered, learn about new book releases, and receive exclusive content!

JOIN THE GROUP NOW:
www.facebook.com/groups/smallbusinesswealthmarketing/

GET YOUR FREE GIFTS HERE:
https://goldspielcreativeenterprises.com/free-gifts-from-likes-to-profits/

ACKNOWLEDGMENTS

Thank you to all of my clients past and present who helped me to learn these skills and more. Without you, the content in this book would not have been possible.

INTRODUCTION

"Social media will help you build up loyalty of your current customers to the point that they will willingly, and for free, tell others about you!"

– Bonnie Sainsbury

"Traditional advertising doesn't work anymore!" That's what a 2015 article by Forbes stated and that sentiment hasn't changed. If anything, it's gotten truer. More and more it's become clear that using traditional advertising to build a business just doesn't work.

Gone are the days when brands could publish an ad in a newspaper and get sales. Heck, traditional newspapers are all but gone these days. Many are now only available digitally online or via apps. The same is true of the traditional use of flyers or even, to some extent, TV ads for advertising brands. These methods just don't work anymore and continuing to use them will only waste your money and time as well as cause immense frustration when they don't get the results your brand is looking for.

So, what is the solution for getting your brand in front of the right audience? Social media! Yet still I see brands, from local eateries to small home businesses to large corporations, not using the right social media platforms for their brand or, worse yet, not using social media at all!

You might be asking right about now, "What's the big deal? Social media is important but it's not the be all and end all." Well…I beg to differ. Here are a few things that your brand is missing out on if you are either not utilizing social media at all or you aren't using the right social media platforms for your brand:

- **TRUST – People will trust your brand less!** A recent study discovered that 63% of respondents look up products and brands on social media before making purchases. If they can't find you, you're invisible to them and your brand means nothing to them. How can they trust a brand if they know nothing about it?
- **POPULARITY – Your brand will be less popular and less likely to gain a consumer following!** Remember those 63% of people above that look up products and brands on social media before making purchases? Well, that same 63% tend to share branded content with their followers! If your brand is not on social media or is not utilizing it correctly, those people won't know about your brand and they'll share your competition's products and services instead.

- **LEADS - You'll get less people contacting you for more information about your brand or service.** Studies have found that 58% of people engage with brands on social media rather than any other point of contact. However, if you're not there or you're on the wrong social media platforms, they can't contact you and bye-bye leads.
- **REFFERAL TRAFFIC - Your brand will be missing out on referral traffic.** The fact is that social media sites have higher daily statistics than most websites. Social media provides access to a huge ocean of potential customers that your website alone can't reach. In fact, most people find brands through social media platforms more than any other way.
- **BRAND INFLUENCE - Your brand's content won't be as effective.** Branded content on social media influences up to 81% of consumers to buy a company's product or service. How can your brand or business have any brand influence if the right people can't find it?
- **ACCESS TO INFLUENCERS - Finding influencers to help promote your brand or service will be virtually impossible.** This is because on social media, influencers run the show and they have huge pools of followers on social media that are waiting to be shown what to purchase next. If your brand or service is not on social media or not on the best platforms to find its ideal customers or clients,

it will have virtually no access to the top influencers and their audience of loyal followers.

- **BRAND RECOGNITION – If you're not where everyone else is, no one will know who you are.** With the majority of the population making purchasing choices through social media platforms, if your brand isn't well represented there, no one will know your products or services enough to give them a chance.

- **PROFITS! – You can't sell to an audience that's not interested in what you've got to offer.** The longer you waste your time and money on platforms that aren't aligned with your business or brand, the more profits you are missing out on.

However, just being on social media is not the complete solution. You have to be on the **CORRECT** social media platforms for your brand or service. If you aren't where your ideal clients or customers are, you might as well not be on social media at all.

That's where this book comes to the rescue because I've done all the hard work for you. In this book I'm going to show you which social media platforms your brand's ideal clients or customers are hanging out on so you don't have to blindly guess and waste your time and money.

However, before we dive into the complexities of choosing social media platforms for your brand, I'd like to tell you a bit about myself.

My journey started back in 2006, when I was hired as an independent contractor for one of the biggest (and TALLEST…hint, hint) personal development coaches in the world. That led to me being recommended to other personal development leaders in the industry as well as other corporations who were looking for my expertise. At that time, my expertise was in the realm of transcription, editing, writing, and other types of content creation.

I was then hired by, and later became business partners with, two chiropractors who were looking to positively change the massage therapy profession. It was through that partnership that my skills really began to expand into product, website, and blog content writing, editing, website development, product development, and social media management. All of which, up to that point, I had never done before. However, I was the most tech savvy of the three of us so it was left to me to figure everything out.

During that time, every step of the creative process turned into a long, arduous ordeal of searching the web for answers that I assumed would be easy to find. I also assumed the answers would be accurate. I was wrong.

I soon found there was no one website or book that I could go to in order to find the answers I needed. Everything I did had to be pieced together bit by bit as I found answers here and there. When all was said and done it turned out that I did everything completely and utterly backwards. As a result, I wound up spending money on things that I either didn't need or that didn't work. This was all because I couldn't find one resource that could take me efficiently and correctly through the processes I needed to master.

In the end, I mottled through and managed to find everything I needed but it took so much longer than it needed to and cost so much more than necessary.

After that enlightening growth experience, word got out about what I had accomplished and I began to be approached by other people who were looking for help with their blogs, websites, and social media campaigns. I started helping people from all over the world, from a European professional poker player to a non-profit bird sanctuary in the United States to various others needing my assistance for their brands.

Soon I was working non-stop helping all these people but there just wasn't enough time in the day to continue this way. That's when, with some encouragement from friends and clients, I realized that I needed to find a better way to help more people in less time. From this, the idea for my first book,

Making Your Business a Social Media Superstar: A Step-by-Step Guide to Creating, Maintaining, and Promoting Your Online Presence was born. That was 2015.

Since that time, I worked as a social media manager at a digital agency where I gained extensive knowledge of social media management as well as how to look at statistical and demographic data to determine the right social media platforms for individual brands and businesses. During that time, I also became a prolific content writer - writing blogs, books, and web content - as well as a creator of dozens of websites and blogs for individuals and organizations. All this while still working as an independent contractor/freelancer for that personal development coach mentioned earlier, which was an experience that not only taught me so much about business and promotion but also about life and human psychology. All of which are extremely helpful to know when choosing social media platforms and knowing how to promote your brand.

In this book, I want to teach you how to choose the best and most profitable social media platforms for your brand. I also want to teach you what you need to know to be an expert in when it comes to knowing where to find your ideal clients so that you can take your brand from likes to profits confidently even when the social media landscape changes, which inevitably it will. After you finish this book, you will have the knowledge required to decide for yourself which platforms have the best ability to grow your business' brand and bank account. By the end of this book, **YOU WILL HAVE THE POWER TO TURN YOUR BRAND'S LIKES INTO PROFITS!**

Throughout this book you will learn about the specific demographics and audiences that each social media platform attracts so that you can confidently choose the ones that are right for you and your brand.

I will also show you my **Top 3 Must-Haves** for every business that are the absolute bare necessity when it comes to creating an online presence. These 3 Must-Haves coupled with the **CORRECT** social media platforms for your brand will start you on the journey to improving your brand's visibility and profits.

A whopping 90% of brands fail on social media because they fail to understand the psychology and demographics of the platforms they chose to be on. Research by the Proxima Group states that $38 billion of worldwide marketing budgets are wasted on poor digital marketing.

My goal in writing this book is to save you and your brand the time, energy, money, and frustration that those brands that failed had to endure and learn the hard way. Once you finish reading this book you will be so far ahead of most brands that are haphazardly choosing social media platforms and wondering why they aren't seeing any profits.

Don't wait another moment! If you're ready to take your brand to the next level by increasing its following, its reputation, and most of all, its cash in the bank then let's get started on the path **FROM LIKES TO PROFITS!**

CHAPTER 1

WHY YOUR ORGANIZATION NEEDS A SOCIAL MEDIA PRESENCE

"Social Marketing eliminates the middleman, providing brands the unique opportunity to have a direct relationship with their customers."

– Bryan Weiner

There are many reasons why a brand needs to have a social media presence though surprisingly I find that many still do not have one. Many people have the mistaken belief that social media is for kids or it's for people with nothing better to do than create posts about their latest meal, their baby's first steps, or their brilliantly original philosophies about life. However, thinking that way can cost you and your brand potential customers or clients.

Having a social media or digital presence online can accomplish a great deal of things for your business. The first of which is spreading the word about your brand's products or services. Let's face it. If people don't know who you are, what you're doing, and how your products or services can benefit them or the world, your intentions, no matter how noble, won't mean a thing. You could have a product that cures cancer 100% of the time with absolutely no negative side effects but if people don't know about it, then it might as well not exist at all.

Creating a social media identity allows you to build a brand and a following of like-minded people who are interested in what you and your business are doing. It's a place where people can find out more about your products, services, and causes. Your brand's social media pages are the places where you detail all the different resources you have as well as what your mission, goals, and visions are so that people have the opportunity to get to know you. The more you post quality content, the more people will remember your business or brand. The more they remember about your business or brand, the sooner you become THE business or brand in their minds as well as to the rest of the world.

Your social media presence also provides your followers with an outlet where they can interact directly with you and your brand. When you create your brand's online presence you're naturally going to try to provide as much information about what you're doing and why. However, it is more than likely that you will inadvertently miss some key information that your followers are looking for. It's really hard when you're running a business and creating a brand to remember all the key talking points that you want to tell people about.

However, when you have a social media presence, you're putting yourself and your organization out there so people can more easily find you and ask about any of those things that you might have overlooked. You're creating an open outlet for communication between your business brand and its current as well as potential clients or customers.

A social media presence helps to build trusted relationships by providing direct access to your business. People will go to your social media profiles, websites, and blogs to find out all the essential details about you and your business but they also go to those places to ask you or your organization all the questions that they couldn't find the answers to as well. Your online presence provides a direct connection between your organization and potential customers, clients, or supporters. When you or someone in your organization monitors these sites regularly, it provides your followers with the confidence that they will get answers to their questions and inquiries every time and that builds a trust and rapport that you can't buy.

One of the greatest advantages of having a social media presence on platforms that are in alignment with your ideal customers is how easy it is to gain new prospects, clients, and customers. Your organization's social media profiles are places where you will be regularly posting information, blogs, questions and answers as well as other important resources for your followers. Doing these types of activities creates an environment that makes it extremely easy for your followers to share everything you post with everyone they know. This constantly increases your circle of influence and attracts a constant flow of new clients or customers to you and your brand. Put quite simply, social media extends your customer reach to an audience that might have never known about you and this creates unlimited potential for your brand.

Imagine what it would do for your business brand if you posted an article about your company, its products and services, and how they can solve your customers' biggest problems or address their grandest desires. What would happen if all your followers shared that post with all of their friends, family, and co-workers? The potential that would create for attracting new customers or clients to your business would be immense.

Creating a social media presence on platforms that are in alignment with your ideal customers also helps to create rapport with people by letting them get to know you and your business. Most people want to feel like they know you and your organization. They want to know that you share common goals or visions with them before they decide to purchase a product or service from your company. It's human nature. No one wants to throw their hard-earned money at a product or service that they know nothing about. You and your brand have to gain your followers' trust and support. Social media can be a powerful way to achieve that goal.

Building rapport then leads to the next goal of having a social media presence and that is that it creates a community or family-type atmosphere for your followers. Once you've let your followers know about you, your brand, and its products or services, they will begin to feel a certain amount of rapport with you. They then will start to feel as though you and everyone who works for you are like family members or friends to them.

Creating that family/community atmosphere connects your followers not only to your business brand but it also connects them with each other. The more you help your followers feel like they belong, the more willing they are to support your business and each other. Not only will they purchase products and services from your business but they will also happily spread the news about those products and services to everyone they know. People, as a rule, want their friends and family to be involved with the things that they find useful or meaningful to them and their lives.

Another massive plus when it comes to having a social media presence in alignment with your brand is that it influences search engine rankings. There is this thing called SEO or Search Engine Optimization. A search engine ranking is a fancy term for how you place in the search engines when someone is looking for something that your business brand produces or sells. For example, if I am looking for a plumber and I search Google for 'Plumber in Miami' the results are going to reflect the people with the highest search engine rankings before anyone else.

How do you get high search engine rankings? One of the things that greatly influences your search engine rankings is your social media presence. Simply put, the more active your business brand is on social media platforms, the stronger your rankings will be when it comes to SEO and the easier it will be for perspective clients or customers to find your business.

Speaking of search engines, although people still regularly use search engines like Google, Bing, Firefox, Duck Duck Go, etc., more than ever they are also searching for businesses and products using social media platforms as search engines to find answers to their questions or problems. If your brand isn't there, new clients or customers won't be able to find you, ultimately reducing the profits you could be banking.

Another thing to keep in mind is that virtually every brand has competition that is vying for their client's or customer's attention. If your brand doesn't have a social media presence or it's on the wrong platform for its ideal audience but your competition is on the correct platform, and most likely they are, you need to be there too. And if, by some miracle, your competition doesn't have a social media presence or they're on the wrong platform for its ideal audience, then it's all the better for you because your brand's social media presence will push its ranking even higher in the search engines. Thus creating an opportunity for you to be THE EXPERT in your chosen field.

For those of you who have purposely chosen not to have a social media presence at all for your brand because you still feel it's a passing phase or that it is in decline, let me assure you that it is not a passing phase or in decline. Social media is not going anywhere any time soon. The types of social media platforms may change and morph over time but the fact is more and more people are on social media platforms in ever increasing amounts of time throughout the day and it's not slowing down any time soon.

It used to be that the best place to find clients or customers for your business was through placing ads in newspapers or on television or radio but in today's fast-paced digital age people are relying more and more on social media to find products, services, and causes that they need and want. They are not reading newspapers, watching TV, or listening to radio in search of these things. Business technologies are forever changing and refusing to change with the times creates an antiquated brand that says your company is unwilling or unable to be cutting edge and adapt. That simple action, or lack thereof, can cost you an abundance of customers or clients, which translates to a loss in profits.

If you're a person who requires some statistics to convince you of the need to not only create a social media presence but also choose the correct platforms for your ideal audience then think about these facts for a while. It used to be that porn (yes, porn) was the number one activity on the web but now social media has taken the first-place lead as the number one activity online.

Another interesting statistic is that 93% of marketers use social media for their businesses. Do you want to be in the small 7% of the marketing population that isn't on social media? Now I am usually not the one to go with the crowd but sometimes there's a reason why everyone is doing the same thing. This is one of those times. If social media wasn't working as a form of marketing for businesses, trust me, no one would be wasting their time on it.

You also might want to take these statistics in and really think about what they could mean for your brand. The average person spends 2 hours and 24 minutes on social media every day. It is estimated that users will spend 4 trillion hours on social media this year alone.

Some other statistics for you:

- 26.6% of users use social media for "Finding inspiration for things to do and buy."
- 25.9% of users use social media for "Finding products to purchase."
- 21.7% of users use social media for "Seeing content from your favorite brands."
- 19.7% of users use social media for "Finding like-minded communities and interest groups."
- 19.6% of users use social media for "Following celebrities or Influencers."

Do you need a few more statistics to convince you of the importance of not only being on social media but also being on the **RIGHT** social media platform for your business brand? How about the fact that **500 MILLION** Tweets on X are sent **EVERY DAY**! (By the way, that's up from 58 million tweets in 2015!) That calculates to around 6,000 tweets being shared per second and 350,000 being shared per minute and that's just on **ONE** social media platform!

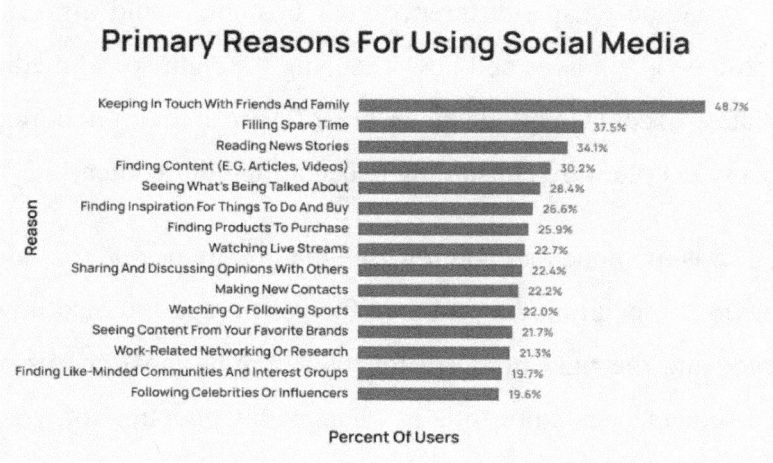

Source: https://explodingtopics.com/blog/social-media-usage
i

Then there's Facebook stats! On average, **350 million** photos are uploaded, **1 BILLION** stories are shared and about **4.75 billion** items are shared every day on Facebook alone!

How about Instagram? Well, on that platform **1.3 billion** photos are shared **every day** which equals just over **900,000** photos **every minute** of every day! (By the way, that's up from only 3,600 every minute of every day in 2015.)[ii]

And just to add a little icing to the cake and hammer the point home, in 2024, there are estimated to be **5.17 billion** total social media users worldwide. With the average person using 6.7 different social platforms per month.[iii]

Imagine what a difference your business could make to those people's lives and how choosing the right social media platform could explode your brand's profit margin if that many people were consuming and sharing your content!

It is my hope that you now see the importance of not only having a social media presence for your brand but also how choosing the right platform for your brand's ideal clients or customers can exponentially change the direction of your business for the better. Social media is more than just likes and comments. Social media should also be about spreading your brand's awareness and turning likes into profits!

CHAPTER 2

TOP 3 MUST-HAVES FOR EVERY BUSINESS

"Social media is about the people! Not about your business. Provide for the people and the people will provide for you."

– Matt Goulart

Before I get down to the nitty gritty details of how to choose the most profitable social media platforms for your brand, I want to show you what I consider to be the Top 3 Must-Haves for every business in order to create a solid online presence. I also want to be clear about the fact that you don't have to be on every single social media platform that's out there. The key is to pick the platforms that are the best fit for your brand and that means strategically picking the ones where your ideal clients or customers are.

It's also important that you only create as many online profiles as are absolutely necessary. Adding more than you need will only frustrate you and make it difficult to maintain and promote on them on a regular basis.

Now my theory for everything in life these days is to keep things as inexpensive and simple as possible. More is definitely not always better and neither is throwing money at things you don't really need. There are plenty of low or no-cost solutions out there that do the things that you need them to do. As your business brand grows you can add services or platforms that cost a bit but only if it's absolutely necessary. You never want to pay for platforms, websites, or social media plugins if there are alternatives available to you that are free or low-cost that can do the same things. Instead keep that money to reinvest into your business.

I firmly believe that for any business you only need three basic things to get started and those three things can carry you a long way before you need to add anything else.   Now some of you reading this are going to be thinking, "What business doesn't have these things in 2024?" and my answer to you is…A LOT! I am constantly amazed at the number of businesses, brands, and artists that do not have one or more of these essential items and then wonder why they're not doing as well as they hoped. I've said it once and I'll say it again, if people can't find you and your business they can't know about your products or services and all their searching for answers will land them on your competition's websites buying their products and services instead of yours.

So here are the Top 3 Must-Haves for every business, brand, and/or artist. In my opinion, at the least, every business, brand, and/or artist should have these 3 things!

#1: A Simple Business Website

Every business, brand, and/or artists needs to have, at least, a simple website. You MUST have a place where you can send prospects where they can learn more about who you are, what you do, and what products or services you provide. If you are selling a product or service, that website needs to, at a minimum, direct potential clients or customers to the place where they can purchase those products or services. You also have to make it easy for them to find that place. Don't lead them on a wild goose chase trying to figure out how to purchase your products or services. If it's too hard to figure out, they're going to head on over to your competition's website and purchase from them. I am amazed sometimes by how many business websites do not clearly show their website visitors how to purchase from them.

Keep in mind that you never want to create a website that overwhelms visitors either. It's best to keep the website clean, simple, and easy to navigate as well as make sure it has all the vital information that visitors need to know in order to take action.

I can't tell you how many times I've gone to a business' website and had to go on a treasure hunt to find out their phone number, address, or business hours. This is basic information that people regularly look for on a website. You never want people spending inordinate amounts of time looking for this type of information. It's frustrating and eventually most people will give up and leave. Not having the most basic information visible for all to see will cost you and your business potential clients or customers, which translates into loss of income!

Your website should contain several key points that are easy for potential clients or customers to find.

First is your homepage. The homepage is basically a digital business card. It is going to have all the basic information mentioned above such as phone number, address, and hours of operation (if applicable). If your business is strictly an online one, then make that clear and provide other ways for visitors to your site to contact you on the homepage. Examples of alternate ways for visitors to contact you would be a link that allows them to email you or message you via apps like WhatsApp or Facebook Messenger, or give them the links to the social media platforms your business or brand is on.

The homepage should also contain attractive pictures as well as a summary of what your business is really about. If your business is selling products or services, then the homepage should have a brief synopsis of what some of those products or services are with a link to more detailed information about each one.

Next, there should be a 'Contact Us' page. This is super important and is in addition to the contact information on the homepage. You want potential customers or clients to be able to freely contact you with questions, comments, or issues whenever they want or need to. Some people would prefer to just put their email address on the homepage and leave it at that but I've learned from experience that doing that can be a mistake. In this day and age, I probably don't need to tell you but I will anyway, there are people out there that LOVE when people post their email address online because it makes it super easy for them to send ongoing, never-ending spam or, worse yet, viruses to your email or computer. If you have to put an email address anywhere on your website, make sure it's a professional email linked to your website hosting company with your URL as part of it. (Example: support@yourwebsite.com) And make sure that the email is protected from spam. Most hosting sites automatically have spam protection enabled on website emails like this.

If you or your business doesn't have an email with your hosting site and you only have an email from Gmail, Yahoo, or some other free email provider, then I would advise you to not post that on your website anywhere. Instead, only use a contact form to enable people to contact you or your business. When using a contact form on your website, you can even put what is called a Captcha on the form in order to prevent bots, computerized spammers, from filling it out. You've probably seen a Captcha many times before when surfing the web. It's one of those little boxes where you have to type a word or sentence into it after either looking at a hard to look at word, watching a video with a clue, or hearing a word spoken out loud. Sometimes they even have you click on boxes that contain pictures of crosswalks or some such. They can be slightly irritating but they help prevent bots from summiting anything through your contact form. I personally find them a little annoying, mostly because I can never get the word right the first time, but they are very effective for keeping your website and email secure.

Next, your website should also contain an 'About Us' page. This is a page where you go more in depth about you, your business, and/or projects. Generally, an 'About Us' page will contain a picture of you and anyone else you feel are top players in your organization along with brief biographies of each person. This is also a great place to put a mission statement and/or your 'Why' for creating your business or brand. This is where your future clients or customers can get to know you and your business better and decide if it is in alignment with their mission and why. It also offers them insights as to whether you or your brand holds the solutions to their problems or desires.

And lastly, if your organization provides services or products, you need a sales page. This page can be made simply with pictures and descriptions of the products or services with a 'Buy Now' button. You don't need a fancy shopping cart solution that costs you tons of money to do this especially if you're just starting out. You can add more expensive solutions as your business grows. In the meantime, there are simple solutions like PayPal, Square, or Stripe (there are many others as well) that can cost-effectively handle this portion of your website easily.

All of these things are easy and low or no-cost to do. If you have all of these suggestions in place that's all you really need to get your business or brand's website off the ground.

#2: A Blog

Now there are two ways you can approach having a blog. You can incorporate it into your website, which most people do, or you can have a separate blog that you can just put a link to on your website.

There really is no right or wrong way. In the past, I wavered between the two options but now I feel that simpler is better, which is to make the blog part of your website. In 2024, creating websites has come a long way and most website platforms, regardless of cost, usually include the blog page as part of every website. Having your blog part of your website saves you the pain of having to sign into two separate places all the time to update blogs and website pages. I am all about keeping it simple and easy. I learned this the hard way through doing things the most difficult and complicated ways possible earlier in my career. So, it's my mission to try and save you from having to go through all that pain and frustration too. I mean, someone should benefit from my experience, right?

Many people feel a blog is unnecessary if they already have a website but I disagree. There is a huge difference between your website and your blog. Websites are more like a business card or brochure of your business or brand. It's where people go to get the cold, hard facts about what you're all about and the information on your website usually doesn't change on a regular basis. It only really changes if there are changes in products or services offered, if there are personnel changes, or if there are changes in your contact information like address, phone number, directions, etc.

I compare a website to a resume. It's the very best of who you are, what you're doing, how you can solve people's problems, and how they can get in touch with you. It's very professional, to the point, and is meant to present the best of who you are and what your business does.

A blog, on the other hand, is more informal. You're still presenting the best of who you are but you're doing it in a more informal and conversational type of setting. On your blog you will be posting articles about your business or brand. You are posting blogs about how your products or services can benefit your clients or customers by solving their problems or making their desires become reality.

Your blog is also the place where you post articles with valuable tips that your followers can do right now to get the results they want or solve a problem they have. It's a place where you can answer commonly asked questions from your customers or clients. It's also a place where you can get more in depth about the services your company provides or the products and solutions you have that will help your clients or customers. You can also write blogs about upcoming events, awards your company has won, products being developed, or trends that are happening in your business' niche.

Blogs are basically the place where you can sit down with your potential clients or customers and really find ways to not only connect with them on an informal and personal level but it's also a place where you can coach them towards achieving their goals and solving their challenges. It's a very freeing and liberating way to communicate with everyone you have contact with and it can do so much good not only for your business but for your followers as well.

Ultimately, your blog should be set up so that anytime you write a new blog post or article it automatically gets sent to all of your social media profiles immediately. This makes it extremely easy to spread the news about your business or brand and it saves you or your social media manager a ton of time when it comes to maintenance and promotion.

#3: A Facebook Business Page

Once you have your website and blog set up, the next thing you want to have set up is your Facebook Business page. This is different from your personal Facebook profile. You never want to use your personal Facebook profile as your business page and there are many reasons for this. This first of which is that Facebook doesn't like when people do that and if they see that you're working your business via a personal profile they might, in the least, contact you and tell you to stop it or, at the worst, shut down your personal profile for good.

When we get to the chapter on Facebook and its demographics, you'll see why I've made this particular social media platform a must for **EVERY** business or brand. This is the only platform that gets this distinct honor from me and you'll see why later in this book.

However, there are other reasons why you want to set up a separate business Facebook page and not use your personal Facebook profile for your business. One of which is limitations. When you set up a personal Facebook profile you can only have a certain number of 'friends' like your page and follow you. Once you reach that level, you cannot add any more.

Limitations like this are not good for a business because you want as many people as possible to follow your business. The more people that like, follow, and share your Facebook content, the better your potential is to reach even more people whom you can help with their problems and who can, in return, help spread the news about your business or brand.

Another reason that this limitation is bad for business is because it can actually cause you to lose the followers you already have. You see, if you use your personal Facebook profile as your business page, when you reach the allowable number of 'friends' on that page you'll likely want to change over and set up a business page where you can have an unlimited number of followers. However, that means that you have to coax all your current 'friends' on your personal page to "Like" your new business page and I can assure you that many just won't do it. Not because they no longer like your business anymore but because they either won't be aware of the switch over or they can't be bothered to like another page.

It's sad but true. Many people just won't do a simple thing like "Like" another page of yours when they've already liked your personal page. Why should they?

Now there are ways of enticing them to follow you over to your new business or brand's page like holding a contest for everyone who "Likes" the page or by giving away some free content to everyone who transfers over to the new business page but it can still be a lot of unnecessary work. Well worth it, but work nonetheless!

A great reason to set up a business Facebook page right from the beginning is because the more followers you get, the more opportunities Facebook gives you to spread the news about your business or brand. You see, once you reach a certain number of followers on your business Facebook page, it opens up new advertising opportunities for your business. Advertising on Facebook allows you to target the precise audience that your business or brand appeals to most, which in turn opens you up to more visibility online and in the major search engines. This is one of those little things that can snowball into a big thing if you do it right from the beginning. You cannot do these types of things with a personal profile on Facebook. Advertising is reserved for business pages.

The good news is that setting up a separate business page on Facebook is incredibly simple and worth the effort to do it right from the start.

Now there are a few practical reasons for not using your personal Facebook profile as a business page too. **The biggest one is called BOUNDARIES!** You never, ever want to mix your personal life with your professional life. Doing so can, at the least, cause your personal life to become an open book to the public, and at worst, damage your reputation as a professional. You do not want strangers on your personal profile knowing everything that's going on in your private life. Save your personal pages for your real close friends and relatives and let everybody else follow your professional business page. Trust me, you will be grateful that you created and maintained those boundaries once your business or brand begins to take off.

Other Social Media Platforms

There are seemingly an unlimited number of social media platforms in the world. Obviously too many to be covered in this book. However, there are about a dozen social media platforms that are globally the most popular. If your business or brand is just starting out then I would advise that you begin with the Top 3 Must-Haves outlined in this chapter and build your social media presence from there. You can increase your search engine rankings, attract more followers, and gain more clients or customers just by having these Top 3 Must-Haves in place, linked together, and ready to go than you can by having profiles on every social media platform out there.

There is no real need to make life any more complicated than that when you're first starting out. I know businesses that have grown and thrived with just these Top 3 Must-Haves. The key to success is not only making sure you set them up properly but also, choosing the most profitable social media platforms for your business and brand. I will go over some of the most popular social media platforms out there in the following chapters.

I also want to emphasize that consistency is key when it comes to social media success. You must regularly add content and engage with all your followers. The more your followers see your business or brand's content in their newsfeeds, the more they will engage with you and share your content with everyone they know.

Now I also want to mention that after reading the following chapters you might be tempted to create social media profiles on all of these platforms regardless of whether they are a perfect match for your business or brand. It's just human nature to have the logic that 'more is better' but that's not usually the case. In most instances, doing this just makes the task of keeping up with regular maintenance and content harder than it really needs to be.

My personal mission and goal of this book is to take the massive amount of information and disinformation regarding the most popular social media platforms out there and boil it down to an easy-to-use, easy-to-choose format. I want you to be able to take the information in this book and make solid, well-informed decisions about which social media platforms will offer your business and/or brand the most bang for the buck. I want you to be able to confidently choose which social media platforms are not only the best fit for your business and/or brand but also which ones are going to be the most profitable!

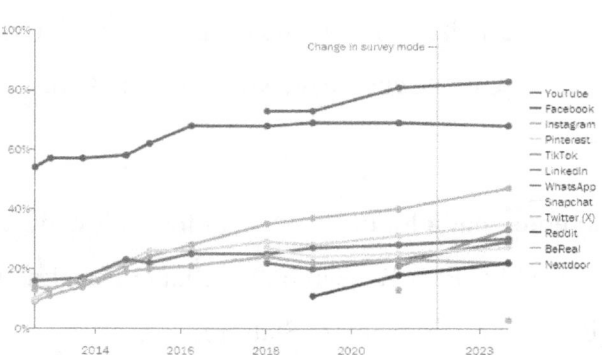

[Source: https://www.pewresearch.org/internet/fact-sheet/social-media]iv

Now it's not possible for me to cover every single social media platform in this book, however, I am going to try and cover the most popular ones that are used today. Many of these platforms are owned by Meta (a.k.a. Facebook). Regardless of that fact, they all attract a different set of demographics such as how many active users are on the platform, as well as their age, gender, location, education level, political affiliation, community type, and financial status. Understanding this information is what will help you decide which platform is right for your business and/or brand. **WELL-EXECUTED KNOWLEDGE LEADS TO PROFITS!**

The next few chapters are going to be filled with statistics and demographics and might feel a bit overwhelming…or…dare I say it, boring. However, I urge you to stick with it because it's only by knowing who you're talking to on all these social media platforms that you can make the best possible choice on where to spend your time and money.

Also note, that a lot of the stats in the following chapters were reported by Pew Research and I have noted as such in the beginning of the chapter. Stats received from any other source will be always be notated. Any stat that is not cited in the following chapters are from Pew Research.

But before we delve into all the stats and demographics, I think it's important to talk about how to know who your ideal clients or customers are.

CHAPTER 3

WHO'S YOUR IDEAL CLIENT OR CUSTOMER?

"Everyone is not your customer."

– Seth Godin

Now before you can decide which social media platforms will be the most profitable for your business or brand, you have to first know who your ideal clients or customers are. Your ideal customers or clients are sometimes referred to as your customer avatars. Customer avatars are also sometimes called "buyer persona" and the purpose of creating this avatar or persona is so you know who your product or services are speaking to. Without knowing who your products are services are appealing to, you have no way of knowing how to reach them more efficiently and directly.

Think about it. You could just pick a couple of your favorite social media platforms to market on and see what happens. Chances are you will probably get some customers or clients from those marketing efforts. Or you could go full out and market on all of the social media platforms. Sure, you'll most likely get a lot of customers or clients from doing that but doing that will also create a lot of work for you or your social media manager. The purpose of this book is to make reaching your ideal customers or clients easier so you can create a more profitable business or brand. If you're not marketing or creating conversations on the right social media platforms, you're just wasting your time and money.

Here's another way to think about it. If your product or service appeals to or benefits 18-year-olds that are getting ready to leave home for the first time to go to college but you're marketing on a social media platform where the majority of users are 65 years old and up, you're just not going to get a lot of interest. That means very little profits.

However, if your products or services appeals to or benefits toddlers and you're marketing and creating conversations on social media platforms where the majority of the users are young moms, then you will definitely be reaching the right customer avatar for your business or brand.

There are two major keys when marketing. The first is you have to know **WHO** your ideal customers or clients are. You need to know everything that you possibly can about them. You need to know who they are, what their pain points and challenges are, and what they need in order to address those pain points and challenges and solve them.

The second major key when marketing is that you need to know **WHERE** your ideal customers or clients are. If your product or services target men between the ages of 39 and 50, who live in the city and make $100,000 or more annually, they are going to hang out in totally different places than women between the ages of 29 and 40, who live in the country, have 5 small children and make $45,000 annually.

Knowing the answer to WHO your ideal avatars are for your business or brand takes a little time to figure out but once you do the work, finding WHERE they are is as simple as staying on top of social media trends.

Once you figure out the WHO and WHERE, you only need to periodically (once or twice a year) review those two things to make sure that 1) your products or services are still targeted at the same audience and 2) that the social media platforms your business or brand is marketing on still attracts your ideal audience.

Now I also want to mention that even if you feel that everything has remained the same as far as your products or services and your ideal customers or clients, it's still a good idea to review the WHO and the WHERE at a minimum once a year. Also, if you've added any new products or services since the last time you reviewed the WHO and WHERE, it's a good idea to revisit the activities in this chapter to make sure they are for the same ideal customer or client. If they are targeting a different audience, then you need to find out where that audience hangs out and make adjustments to your marketing plan to accommodate them.

STEP ONE:
Identifying Your Ideal Customers or Clients

There are many ways to learn more about your ideal customers or clients. If your business or brand is just starting out and you don't yet have any customers or clients, you might be wondering how the heck you're supposed to know who they are. The answer is that regardless of whether you have customers or clients already or not, the method is the same!

LIST YOUR PRODUCTS AND SERVICES

The first step to identifying your ideal customers or clients is to know what you're trying to sell them. You are going to sit down either by yourself (if you're a lone wolf in your business) or with your team and you are going to think about all the products or services your business or brand offers. Then you are going to write all of those products or services you offer down. Every last one of them.

Once you've written all the products and services down that your business or brand offers, you're going to think about WHO each of those products or services are for. In doing this, you might find that those products or services are split between different demographics. That's okay. Knowing that will help you decide not only who to market them to but also where to market each of them. It just means that you might have to do a little extra work by creating several marketing campaigns to several different social media platforms. It's a little more work but it will be well worth it. Now if all your products or services appeal to the same type of people, that's wonderful too especially if you're a new business because you only have to concentrate on that one audience and finding the best social media platforms for that audience.

START ASKING QUESTIONS

The next step to uncovering your business or brand's ideal customer or client (A.K.A. customer avatar) is to start asking questions. Lots of questions. This may seem like a waste of time to some of you but I assure you it is not. The only way to find your ideal customer avatar is to know who they are and the only way to know who they are is to ask questions.

Now if your business or brand is just starting out and you don't really have any customers or clients yet, you're going to have to use your imagination to visualize who the ideal customers or clients are for the products or services you are providing.

For example, if your one of the products your business or brand sells is baby christening outfits, that is a product that is aimed at a specific audience. Who is that audience? Is that audience predominately male or female? My educated guess says it's probably a female dominated audience. Some men might be looking for this item but usually it's the mother, godmother, or grandmother who is looking for this particular item.

How old is your ideal customer or client? In this case, although the product itself, the christening outfit, is intended for a child that's usually a few months old or less, the audience you're most likely aiming for is usually in the 18- to 39-year-old age category for the mothers and probably 39+ for the godmother or grandmother. So, the age range of this audience is pretty wide – 18 to 80+ years old. This is great to know. So now you know that your audience is predominately women ages 18 years old and up!

Next you might want to know how much your ideal customer or client makes per year so you know whether they can afford to purchase your product. If you sell high-end christening outfits that are made of the finest silk with gold lace that has to be pre-ordered and shipped from directly from Rome, then you're going to want to make sure that you target your marketing towards people in the financial income categories that are most likely able to afford something like that.

And you just keep asking yourself these questions, one after the other, and writing down the specifics of who needs, wants, or can afford your products or services until you get a crystal-clear vision of who your ideal customers or clients are.

Here's another example for you. If your company or brand sells website creation services, then ask yourself who are your ideal customers. Now you might be tempted to say, "Well, my client is everyone." And maybe that's true but that audience is too large and complicated to market to especially if you're a small business or just starting out. Who are you really creating websites for? Who were you thinking of when you created your business or brand? A lot of times we create products or services that we, ourselves, need and then want to provide that product or services to others like us. So, who are you then? Are you a woman? A man? How old are you? What are the unique challenges or pain points that you want solved?

Or maybe the product or service your business or brand created is not aimed at people like yourself. Maybe you created that product or service to help a friend or colleague. Who are those people that you created that product or service for? What solutions are they looking for? How much do they earn annually? How old are they?

The way to find out who your ideal customers or clients are is to ask as many questions as possible so that you get a very clear and concise vision of that individual or group. Some even go so far as to name that ideal customer or client and describe what they look like and what their average day looks like. That isn't always necessary but the more detailed you can get about who your ideal customer is, the easier it will be to figure out which social media platforms they hang out on among other things.

Here is a list of characteristics you should identify when trying to figure out who your ideal customer or clients are:

- **Age** – How old is your ideal customer or client?
- **Gender** – Are they predominately male, female, a good mixture of both?
- **Marital Status** – Are your ideal clients married, divorced, single, widowed? Individuals in these different marital categories make very different decisions.
- **Number of Children** – Do they have 1 child, 5 children, no children?
- **Race/Ethnicity/Religion** – These differences can make a bit difference when choosing products or services. For example, if you're selling the christening outfits mentioned above, then your audience most likely is NOT

anyone who's Jewish, Muslim, or anything other than Christian.

- **Income** – Like I mentioned above, if your product or service is high-end, you need to know that your audience is not people who are just barely scraping by and having trouble meeting their family's needs UNLESS your product or service addresses that particular issue or challenge in some way.
- **Occupation** – What does your ideal customer or client do for a living? If you're selling a product or service that helps large businesses or corporations, you're not going to market to home-based businesses.
- **Location** – Is your product or service location-based? If so, you need to be aware of this. If not, then this one may not matter at all.
- **Goals** – What are their goals and values? What do they want out of life?
- **Life Stage** – If your product or service is aimed at 18–29-year-olds, you don't want to market on a social media platform that predominately attracts people 65+ years old.
- **Psychographics** – What hobbies, attitudes, beliefs, or interests do they have?
- **Other information** – What do they read? What podcasts do they listen to?
- **Pain Points and Challenges** – What problems or challenges are they looking to find a solution to? What

keeps them up at night? Knowing these things not only helps target the audience for your current products or service but can also help you determine new products or services to meet their needs.

Then you need to find the answers to these more in-depth questions as well:

- *What does your product or service accomplish from your customer's point of view?*
- *What are the specific benefits your customer is seeking in buying your product or service?*
- *When does your ideal customer buy your product or service?*
- *What would be your ideal customer or client's objections to buying your product or service?*
- *What products, services, or methods did your ideal customer or client already try that didn't work and is the reason they are coming to you for a solution? Is what you have to offer something totally new that hasn't been tried before?*

If you already have some customers or clients, the process is the same as above but you have a few extra ways to get this information and more. The biggest way is to just ask your current customers or clients these questions directly.

Here are a few ways to easily do that:

- **Surveys** – Send your customers surveys by mail or email, use comment cards, have a survey on your website, create surveys that you share on your social media pages.
- **Customer Focus Groups** – Get some of your best customers together and ask them questions. This works great if you can do it locally but you can also do this via a video call using Zoom or Microsoft Teams, etc.
- **Social Media** – Do some research on social media to see what customers are saying about your business or service.
- **Reviews** – The internet is a great source of information if you use it properly. Check out your business or brand's online ratings and reviews. You can get a lot of information about what your business or brand is doing right and what it's doing wrong as well as what products or services your customers or clients would love for you to offer them. If you have some bad reviews, use them to improve your current products or services.
- **Talk to Customers** – When you have a customer or client there with you either in person, on the phone, or on a video call, ask them questions. This is the best way to find out how your business or brand is doing and what services or products your customers want and need.

Now if your business products or services are targeted towards other businesses (B2B) then there are different characteristics to identify in order to figure out who your ideal customers or clients are.

Here are just a few to get you started:

- **Industry** – This is very basic information that you should always know. What industry does your ideal customer or client belong to?
- **Job Title** – If your product or service is aimed at a specific person in a corporation, what is their position in that organization? Are they regular employees or are they in the C-Suite (CEO, COO, CFO, etc.)?
- **Locations** – Where are these businesses located? Do they have multiple locations? Are they primarily in cities, suburban areas, or rural areas?
- **Sales/Revenues** – How much do the make every year? Are they doing well and growing or are they floundering and trying to stay afloat?
- **Years in Business** – How long have they been around? Are they new to the industry or do they have a long, successful history? Are they considered leaders in their industry or are they barely known?
- **Number of Employees** – How many employees do they currently have? Are they currently hiring or are they laying people off?

- **Marketing Budget** – How much do they have in their marketing budget? Are they flush with marketing cash or are they very tight when it comes to marketing?
- **Social Media Usage** – Do they use social media as a platform for marketing their brand or business? If so, which platforms do they use most? How frequently do they post? Do they interact with their followers or do questions go unanswered on their social media pages?
- **Challenges or Pain Points** – What are some of the challenges their business, brand, or industry face regularly? What are some of their pain points? Can your business or brand address any of those challenges and provide solutions?

Now a lot of these questions you might be able to answer quite easily if you already have a customer or client base. Usually these are the types of information you gather on a company when they become customers or clients so you might not have to dig too far to find answers. However, if you're a new business or brand and you do not have this information on hand yet, you will have to do some research as well as think about the answers to these questions so you know who you want to market to and who your ideal customers or clients are.

If your business or brand already has come customers or clients then you can do as I've already suggested and ask your customers or clients some questions directly.

Here are a few questions to ask them to get you started:

- *How does your business typically learn about products or services like mine?*
- *Why did you decide to purchase from my business or brand the first time?*
- *Why do you keep doing business with my business or brand?*
- *What do you get from doing business with my company that my competitors don't offer?*
- *How do you use our product or service?*
- *Who do you consider our direct competition?*
- *Do we meet your expectations completely or are there areas where you feel we could improve more?*
- *Is there a service or product that we don't yet offer that you wish we would offer?*
- *Who do you feel our best customers or clients would be? Describe them to me?*

Once you've answered these questions and have done some research, you should have a much clearer picture of who your ideal customer or client (a.k.a. ideal avatar) is and what they want, need, and hope for when it comes to your products or services.

Now we can move on to WHERE to find your ideal customer or clients so that you can start a conversation with them and make your business or brand known to them. They are looking for you but you have to be where they are in order to reach them.

STEP TWO:

Identifying WHERE Your Ideal Customers or Clients Hang Out

As I've said several times already, if you're not where your ideal customers or clients are they can't find you and if they can't find you, they will find your direct competitors. Your direct competitors might not have the best product or service for them or even directly address your ideal customers' or clients' pain points and challenges head on but if you're not there, who else does your ideal customer or client have to go to for solutions? No one! Why? Because you're not there to show them what you can do for them.

In step one I showed you how to clearly define who your ideal customers or clients are by asking yourself and your current customer or clients lots of questions. Now you're going to learn how to figure out WHERE those ideal customers or clients are hanging out. We want to find out which social media platforms are best for finding your ideal customers or clients.

We do this by researching the current demographics for each social media platform and matching that information to the characteristics of your ideal customer avatar that you've just uncovered.

Now you need to know that this isn't a one and done solution. Demographics change regularly. Those changes can be fueled by everything from socioeconomic factors to social unrest to the health of the economy as well as demographic groups entering new life stages. Other things that can affect the audience of social media platforms are changes in the management of the platform as well as changes in algorithms and rules put forth by the platform as well as government agencies. This is why even after you have found out where your ideal customer or clients hang out on social media, you still have to revisit the questions of who they are and where they hang out at least once, if not twice, a year.

So where do we find this demographic information? There are many places online to find demographic information but I would advise you to find reputable sources and return to those sources each time. This will make sure that your demographic information is as accurate as possible as well as queue you into any trends or changes as they happen. If you go to sources that aren't legitimate it's easy for them to make stuff up to suit their needs rather than to inform their audience of the actual facts.

These are some of the sources that I have always relied on for accurate demographics year after year:

- **Statista** (www.statista.com): Statista not only updates their demographic information yearly on social media platforms but they have demographic statistics on just about every industry or subject you can think of. I find them extremely reliable and their methods for finding demographic information year after year are consistent and accurate.
- **Pew Research Center** (www.pewresearch.org): Most of the demographic information for this book was found on Pew Research Center's website or Statista's website. Like Statista, Pew Research Center uses the highest methodological standards and research methods to compile their demographics and statistics. Like Statista, they update this information regularly to keep the demographics as accurate as possible.
- **Sprout Social** (www.sproutsocial.com): Although I prefer to get my demographic information from the first two on this list, sometimes you can't find exactly what you're looking for or there's something missing from the

demographics that you're interested in. When this happens, I seek out knowledgeable social media agencies who seem to have their demographics dialed in to what's trending and happening in the world. Sprout Social is one of those resources that I use often.

- **Forbes** (www.forbes.com): Forbes is one of those dependable resources that has access to virtually every aspect of business and the economy. They regularly, usually once a year, update and publish a list of top social media statistics and trends for the year. It usually comes out during the first six months of the year and I find their demographics fairly on par with other resources on this list.

- **Smart Insights** (www.smartinsights.com): Smart Insights is a digital marketing firm that usually has up to date demographics on all sorts of marketing topics including social media marketing. They usually get their stats from other sources as well as their own but they generally will site those sources in their articles. I frequently will use their articles to find other sources of statistics and demographics.

- **Back Linko** (www.backlinko.com): Back Linko is a new resource that I referenced a few times in this book. I found that they had some statistics and demographic information that others were lacking. However, I also found that sometimes their demographic information conflicted with

Statista and Pew Research, my main sources of demographic information, and I think that has to do with the fact that they compiled information based on their own research, customer base, and algorithms. One such conflict that I found is their age ranges didn't line up with Statista and Pew Research age ranges. This caused a few discrepancies when looking for information. Still, they had some information that I couldn't find elsewhere so when I used their demographics, I cited them specifically.

Those are the sources I have used most often over the years, and especially when writing this book, to find up to date demographics and statistics on social media platforms and their users. There are plenty of other resources out there that I am sure are just as reliable but these are the ones I find myself going back to over and over. I would suggest when you start your yearly or bi-yearly research, that you start with these resources first and go from there.

Be aware of your resources though. Many of the resources out there are digital marketing agencies that have their own algorithms based on their unique customer-base, which may skew the results somewhat especially when you're trying to find accurate stats on world-wide social media usage. Just always be aware of that. Also, be aware that because some of these resources are digital marketing agencies, they are selling their products and services so they could somewhat skew their demographic information to attract their ideal customers or clients. So, take it all with a grain of salt and trust your gut when it comes to this type of information.

As a general rule, I tend to stick with the information provided by Statista and Pew Research over other sources. If there's a conflict between a source I am looking at and Statista or Pew Research, I will almost always go with Statista or Pew Research. The reason being that they are not digital marketing agencies. They are institutions that are all about research, demographics, and statistics. Pew Research describes themselves as "a nonpartisan fact tank that informs the public about the issues, attitudes, and trends shaping the world." Statista describes themselves as "a global data and business intelligence platform with an extensive collection of statistics, reports, and insights on over 80,000 topics from 22,500 sources in 170 industries." I consider both of these to be reliable resources.

In the next chapters I am going to review the current (2024) demographics for the most popular social media platforms. Each chapter will consist of a list of demographics and statistics and a summary of what that information tells you about that specific platform. Now that you know who your ideal customer or client is, as you read each chapter, see if your ideal customer or client would be an active user on that platform.

Once you're done reviewing the demographics of each social media platform, you should have a pretty good idea which platforms would most likely be the most profitable ones based on your business or brand's ideal customer or client.

Let's start your journey to choosing the most profitable social media platforms for your brand. So, without further ado, let's delve into the different social media platforms and start you on the road from **LIKES TO PROFITS!**

CHAPTER 4

X (FORMERLY KNOWN AS TWITTER)

"Every contact we have with a customer influences whether or not they'll come back. We have to be great every time or we'll lose them."

- Kevin Stirtz

DEMOGRAPHICS:

- ❖ **Active Users:** X has 250 million daily active users and 500 million monthly active users.[v] It is the 5th largest social media platform in the world.
- ❖ **Age:**
    - o 42% of people aged 18-29 use X
    - o 27% of people aged 30-49 use X
    - o 17% of people aged 50-64 use X
    - o 6% of people aged 65+ use X
- ❖ **Gender:**
    - o Among the U.S. population, 26% of males and only 19% of females use X.
    - o Among users of X, 66.72% are male and 33.28% are females.[vi]

- **Location:**[vii]
  - **United States** – the U.S. has the largest proportion of X users with 19.43%.
  - **Japan** – Japan has the second largest proportion of X users with 16.01%.
  - **India** – India's proportion of X users is 4.86%.
  - **United Kingdom** – U.K.'s proportion of X users is 4.79%.
  - **Turkey** – Turkey's proportion of X users is 4.63%.
  - **All Others** – All other countries make up the remaining proportion of X users at 49.72%.
- **Education Level:**
  - 15% of people with a high school level education or less use X.
  - 24% of people with some education at the college level use X.
  - 29% of people with an education beyond the college level, meaning they have graduate or terminal degrees, use X.
- **Financial Status:**
  - 18% of people who earn less than $30,000 use X
  - 21% of people who earn between $30,000 to $69,999 use X

- 20% of people who earn between $70,000 to $99,999 use X
- 29% of people who earn $100,000+ use X

❖ **Race & Ethnicity:**
- 20% of people who are White use X.
- 23% of people who are Black use X.
- 25% of people who are Hispanic use X.
- 37% of people who are English-speaking Asian use X.

❖ **Community:**
- 25% of people who live in an urban area use X.
- 26% of people who live in a suburban area use X.
- 13% of people who live in a rural area use X.

❖ **Political Affiliation:**
- 20% of people who are Republican or Lean Republican use X.
- 26% of people who are Democrat or Lean Democrat use X.

What this all tells us:

X (formerly known as Twitter…I wonder how long it will be before we can stop adding that 'formerly known as' moniker…but I digress) has over 500 million monthly active users and about half of those use X daily. X is the 5th largest social media platform in the world and is not usually one of my first choices for my clients or myself. There are many reasons for that. Some are personal but most are due to the fact that I find X very limiting and, as a social media manager, even before the change from Twitter to X, I never found that there was any worthwhile ROI when using the platform. You have very limited space for messaging and I have never found X/Twitter to have any real benefits for my clients. It just always feels like wasted energy put in the wrong direction. I'm not saying you shouldn't use X but it really shouldn't be one of the top three you should choose, in my opinion, unless the demographics speak directly to your business or brand.

When it comes to age, if you're trying to reach people 50 years old and up, X really isn't the platform for that. Even for ages 30-49, it's not a great match. If you're trying to reach the younger age groups under 30 years old, then X could be a decent extra social media platform to use but I still wouldn't give it top three status.

With gender, X appeals predominately to males. So, if you are trying to reach a mostly male demographic it might be worthy to add X to the mix but, again, I think you can do better platform-wise.

As for location of users, the majority of X's users (about 37%) are in the United States and Japan. The rest of X's users are scattered throughout the world with most countries having about 4-5% of X's demographics. If you're looking to have a world-wide reach, where you touch a small percentage of everywhere, then X could possibly help you reach this goal.

As far as education level, a little more than half of X's users have at least a little college education or an education beyond college (A.K.A. a terminal degree such as a doctorate or PhD). So, X users are a bit more educated than some other social media platforms.

Financially, 70% of X users make $30,000 - $100,000+ a year, which makes them pretty a great audience if you want to make sure your brand gets in front of people who have the means to purchase your products or services.

X users' Race and Ethnicity and Community are pretty evenly distributed with English-Speaking Asians having a slight lead on the white, black, and Hispanic and more X users living in Urban or Suburban communities than rural areas.

X user's affiliation between Republican or Democrat is fairly evenly distributed so there's no real lean towards one side or the other.

X tends to be a social media platform where you can keep up with trends and get news in real-time for up-to-date coverage.[viii] So, it's more of an informational platform as opposed to one that will get you more sales or clients. It's a place to find out what trends are booming and what trends are no longer in. This is more a platform to be a part of so you can see what's happening and what types of products or services are trending so you can keep ahead of your competition.

CHAPTER 5

INSTAGRAM

"The only certain means of success is to render more and better service than is expected of you, no matter what your task may be."

-Og Mandino

DEMOGRAPHICS:

- ❖ **Active Users:** 2 billion monthly active users (MAUs) and approximately 500,000+ daily active users.[ix] It is the 3rd largest social media platform in the world.
- ❖ **Age:**
    - o 78% of people aged 18-29 use Instagram
    - o 59% of people aged 30-49 use Instagram
    - o 35% of people aged 50-64 use Instagram
    - o 15% of people aged 65+ use Instagram
- ❖ **Gender:** 39% of men and 54% of women use Instagram.

- ❖ **Location:**[x]
    - o **India** – 358.55 million Instagram users.

- **United States** – 158.45 million Instagram users.
- **Brazil** – 122.9 million Instagram users.
- **Indonesia** – 104.8 million Instagram users.
- **Turkey** – 56.7 million Instagram users.
- **Japan** – 54.95 million Instagram users.
- **Mexico** – 45.8 million Instagram users.
- **Germany** – 31.55 million Instagram users.
- **United Kingdom** – 31.3 million Instagram users.
- **Italy** – 28.9 million Instagram users.

❖ **Education Level:**
- 37% of people with a high school level education or less use Instagram.
- 50% of people with some education at the college level use Instagram.
- 55% of people with an education beyond the college level, meaning they have graduate or terminal degrees, use Instagram.

❖ **Financial Status:**
- 37% of people who earn less than $30,000 use Instagram
- 46% of people who earn between $30,000 to $69,999 use Instagram
- 49% of people who earn between $70,000 to $99,999 use Instagram

- o 54% of people who earn $100,000+ use Instagram

❖ **Race & Ethnicity:**
  - o 43% of people who are White use Instagram.
  - o 46% of people who are Black use Instagram.
  - o 58% of people who are Hispanic use Instagram.
  - o 57% of people who are English-speaking Asian use Instagram.

❖ **Community:**
  - o 53% of people who live in an urban area use Instagram.
  - o 49% of people who live in a suburban area use Instagram.
  - o 38% of people who live in a rural area use Instagram.

❖ **Political Affiliation:**
  - o 43% of people who are Republican or Lean Republican use Instagram.
  - o 53% of people who are Democrat or Lean Democrat use Instagram.

What this all tells us:

Instagram has about 2 billion monthly active users and about a quarter of those users are on the platform daily. Instagram is the 3rd largest social media platform in the world.

Like Facebook, Instagram is owned by Meta and it is primarily a photo and video sharing social networking service.

The majority of the people (78%) who use Instagram are between the ages of 18-29, followed by (59%) who are between the ages of 30-49. So, you will mostly reach Gen Z and Millennials on this platform.

When it comes to gender, you will mostly reach women on Instagram. They are the number one user of this platform however, keep in mind that women, a.k.a. moms,[xi] make most of the buying decisions in the household. So, this could be a very good platform if your products or services are aimed at women or at household functions, in particular.

India has the most users of Instagram but, again, as with most social media platforms, that's to be expected given the population of that country. After India, however, the United States and Brazil are the top users of the platform making this a great place for U.S. businesses and brands to advertise their products and services.

Instagram is also one of the top platforms where the education demographics indicate that most users have some type of college education. In fact, 55% of the population with an education beyond college, meaning they have a terminal degree like a doctorate or PhD, use the Instagram platform. This makes Instagram a great place to be if your products or services are aimed at that highly educated population. It also means you need to be extremely smart in your advertising here. Populations with this type of educational background aren't going to go for mindless marketing or switch bait tactics like the general population might be lured into. They will be much more critical of marketers and expect a higher standard from products or services marketed here.

As for financial status, the majority of the population that uses Instagram make $70,000 or more in annual income. This is a pretty wealth demographic. So, this platform is a great place to market higher-end products or services. Just make sure you are offering quality products and solutions in exchange for the higher cost or you will lose this audience to a competitor who treats them and their money more respectfully.

As for race and ethnicity, Instagram is fairly evenly distributed among the various groups with a slight advantage aimed towards the Hispanic and English-speaking Asian demographic. Overall, this platform is pretty homogeneous and would reach most races and ethnicities.

Most Instagram users are in suburban or urban areas with a small demographic living in rural areas. This means that if your products or services are aimed at those in rural areas such as farmers, this is probably not the best platform for you to market on because it will not give you the return on investment (ROI) that you're most likely looking for.

Lastly, when it comes to political affiliation, Instagram users are fairly evenly distributed between the two major political parties here in the U.S. with a slight lean (very slight) towards the Democratic side. I don't see this slight lean being that much of an advantage one way or the other though as the percentage difference is so low and there is always room for give one way or the other when it comes to statistics.

CHAPTER 6

PINTEREST

"You are allowed to do this, don't worry about the rules, don't worry about getting into trouble, your job is to take care of the customer, your job is to make that person leave happy. And you have all kinds of leeway to do that."

-John Pepper

DEMOGRAPHICS:

- ❖ **Active Users:** Pinterest had 498 million monthly active users[xii], Pinterest is the 7th largest social media platform in the world.
- ❖ **Age:**
  - o 45% of people aged 18-29 use Pinterest
  - o 40% of people aged 30-49 use Pinterest
  - o 33% of people aged 50-64 use Pinterest
  - o 21% of aged 65+ use Pinterest
- ❖ **Gender:** 19% of men and 50% of women use Pinterest.

- **Location:**[xiii]
  - **United States** – 95 million users
  - **Europe** – 124 million users
  - **Rest of the World** – 246 million users
- **Education Level:**
  - 26% of people with a high school level education or less use Pinterest.
  - 42% of people with some education at the college level use Pinterest.
  - 38% of people with an education beyond the college level, meaning they have graduate or terminal degrees, use Pinterest.
- **Financial Status:**
  - 27% of people who earn less than $30,000 use Pinterest
  - 34% of people who earn between $30,000 to $69,999 use Pinterest
  - 35% of people who earn between $70,000 to $99,999 use Pinterest
  - 41% of people who earn $100,000+ use Pinterest
- **Race & Ethnicity:**
  - 36% of people who are White use Pinterest.
  - 28% of people who are Black use Pinterest.
  - 32% of people who are Hispanic use Pinterest.

- o 30% of people who are English-speaking Asian use Pinterest.

❖ **Community:**
- o 31% of people who live in an urban area use Pinterest.
- o 36% of people who live in a suburban area use Pinterest.
- o 36% of people who live in a rural area use Pinterest.

❖ **Political Affiliation:**
- o 35% of people who are Republican or Lean Republican use Pinterest.
- o 35% of people who are Democrat or Lean Democrat use Pinterest.

What this all tells us:

With 498 million monthly active users, Pinterest is the 7th largest social media platform in the world. Pinterest describes itself as "a visual discovery engine for finding ideas like recipes, home and style inspiration, and more." As you can see by that description, Pinterest is a way for users to find ideas to spark inspiration. It's an idea platform really.

Its users are primarily between the ages of 18-49 years old and although there are Pinterest users over the age of 65 years old, they are the smallest demographic on this platform at only 21%.

Pinterest attracts mostly women to its platform but that's to be expected considering its self-described affiliation with "recipes, home and style inspiration." There are men on this platform but they are a minority and the visual and creative aspect of this social media destination tends to attract more women to it.

As for the location of its users, Pinterest overwhelmingly attracts users from the United States and Europe. Therefore, this platform is great for U.S. and European businesses and brands that are trying to reach their home demographics. It is also great for businesses and brands from other continents who are looking to expand to the U.S. and European markets with their services and products.

When it comes to education, most of Pinterest's users have had at least some college education.

Financially, Pinterest users are fairly evenly distributed among all financial backgrounds with users making $100,000 or more having a slight advantage here but not by much. Products and services of all price ranges and reach would do equally well here.

Demographics for race and ethnicity, community, and political affiliation are all equally distributed among Pinterest users making this platform good for any of these groups.

One big thing to consider here is that Pinterest is a very

visual platform as is Instagram, so your products and services need to be represented in such a way that is visually pleasing when using these platforms or they are likely not going to get much traction here.

CHAPTER 7

LINKEDIN

"You can have everything in life you want if you will just help enough other people get what they want."

-Zig Ziglar

DEMOGRAPHICS:

- ❖ **Active Users:** 1 billion members in 200 countries and regions worldwide.[xiv] LinkedIn is the 9th most popular social media platform in the world.
- ❖ **Age:**
    - o 32% of people aged 18-29 use LinkedIn
    - o 40% of people aged 30-49 use LinkedIn
    - o 31% of people aged 50-64 use LinkedIn
    - o 12% of people aged 65+ use LinkedIn
- ❖ **Gender:** 31% of men and 29% of women use LinkedIn
- ❖ **Location:**[xv]
    - o **United States** – 211 million users
    - o **India** - 117 million users

- o **Brazil** – 70 million users
- o **Indonesia** – 25 million users
- o **Canada** – 22 million users
- o **Mexico** – 21 million users

❖ **Education Level:**
- o 10% of people with a high school level education or less use LinkedIn.
- o 28% of people with some education at the college level use LinkedIn.
- o 53% of people with an education beyond the college level, meaning they have graduate or terminal degrees, use LinkedIn.

❖ **Financial Status:**
- o 13% of people who earn less than $30,000 use LinkedIn
- o 19% of people who earn between $30,000 to $69,999 use LinkedIn
- o 34% of people who earn between $70,000 to $99,999 use LinkedIn
- o 53% of people who earn $100,000+ use LinkedIn

❖ **Race & Ethnicity:**
- o 30% of people who are White use LinkedIn.
- o 29% of people who are Black use LinkedIn.
- o 23% of people who are Hispanic use LinkedIn.

- o 45% of people who are English-speaking Asian use LinkedIn.

❖ **Community:**
- o 31% of people who live in an urban area use LinkedIn.
- o 36% of people who live in a suburban area use LinkedIn.
- o 18% of people who live in a rural area use LinkedIn.

❖ **Political Affiliation:**
- o 29% of people who are Republican or Lean Republican use LinkedIn.
- o 34% of people who are Democrat or Lean Democrat use LinkedIn.

What this all tells us:

With one billion active users in 200 countries and regions worldwide, LinkedIn is the world's 9th most popular social media platform. It is primarily a platform used for strengthening professional relationships as well as finding job or career positions and advise. I consider LinkedIn to be an extension of your professional resume or work experience and a place where you go to connect with professionals in your area of expertise. Although businesses do advertise on LinkedIn, it's not really intended for that purpose and honestly, I've never seen much of an ROI on advertising there.

Now that's not to say no business or brand will do well advertising on LinkedIn, it's just not the best use of marketing dollars in my opinion unless your business is human capital. Then you might do well to market here.

Age-wise, LinkedIn is fairly evenly distributed among the age groups with the least likely age group here being those over 65 years old. That's hardly a shocking statistic considering the platform is mostly used to connect professionally to advance your career. Those over 65 years old are retired or in the process of winding down their professional careers so they are the least likely to use the platform.

When it comes to gender, LinkedIn users are equally divided between male and female genders.

As for location of LinkedIn's users, most users are located in the United States with India coming in second among users. Clearly this platform is more of a U.S.-based social media platform so it's a great place for U.S. businesses or brands to market or for business or brands in other countries that wish to reach a predominately U.S.-based audience.

Not surprisingly, considering the platform's professional career-based users, the majority of LinkedIn's users have college degrees or even terminal degrees, which makes this platform's users highly educated!

And based on the education of LinkedIn's users, it's not surprising that 53% of its users make $100,000 or more annually. Not only are users educated, they are also fairly well-to-do as well. This means that they will most likely be very decerning when it comes to marketers so as a business or brand you need to be on your top game if you want to play here.

As for race and ethnicity, the demographics are fairly evenly distributed among the various groups with English-speaking Asians having a slight lead here but not by much. I would say it's statistically negligible.

Most of LinkedIn's user base are located in either suburban or urban locales with very few located in rural areas. This is to be expected when you consider that most high-paying careers are located in cities or suburban areas and not rural locations.

When it comes to political affiliation, demographically users are fairly evenly split between the democrats and republican groups.

CHAPTER 8

YOUTUBE

"A brand for a company is like a reputation for a person. You earn reputation by trying to do hard things well."

-Jeff Bezos

DEMOGRAPHICS:

- ❖ **Active Users:** YouTube has 2.7 billion users[xvi] and is the 2nd largest social media platform in the world.
- ❖ **Age:**
    - o 93% of people aged 18-29 use YouTube
    - o 92% of people aged 30-49 use YouTube
    - o 83% of people aged 50-64 use YouTube
    - o 60% of people aged 65+ use YouTube
- ❖ **Gender:** 82% of men and 83% of women use YouTube
- ❖ **Location:**[xvii]
    - o **India** – 462 million users
    - o **United States** – 239 million users
    - o **Western Europe** – 162.6 million users
    - o **Brazil** – 144 million users

- **Indonesia** – 139 million users
- **Mexico** – 83.1 million users
- **Japan** – 78.6 million users

❖ **Education Level:**
- 74% of people with a high school level education or less use YouTube.
- 85% of people with some education at the college level use YouTube.
- 89% of people with an education beyond the college level, meaning they have graduate or terminal degrees, use YouTube.

❖ **Financial Status:**
- 73% of people who earn less than $30,000 use YouTube
- 83% of people who earn between $30,000 to $69,999 use YouTube
- 86% of people who earn between $70,000 to $99,999 use YouTube
- 89% of people who earn $100,000+ use YouTube

❖ **Race & Ethnicity:**
- 81% of people who are White use YouTube.
- 82% of people who are Black use YouTube.
- 86% of people who are Hispanic use YouTube.
- 93% of people who are English-speaking Asian use YouTube.

❖ **Community:**
    o 85% of people who live in an urban area use YouTube.
    o 85% of people who live in a suburban area use YouTube.
    o 77% of people who live in a rural area use YouTube.
❖ **Political Affiliation:**
    o 82% of people who are Republican or Lean Republican use YouTube.
    o 84% of people who are Democrat or Lean Democrat use YouTube.

What this all tells us:

Now YouTube, in my opinion, is a superstar when it comes to demographic reach and is one of the top social media platforms that I would recommend to anyone looking to reach A LOT of potential clients or customers. In the past, YouTube wasn't this much of a leader but things have changed since my first book back in 2015.

YouTube has 2.7 billion users and is the 2nd largest social media platform in the world. As I think you will see from their demographic reach, this social media platform just about reaches every type and shape of audience and not in a small way either. It reaches the masses. So, if you can figure out a way for your business or brand to create quality video content that can be consumed on YouTube, I HIGHLY recommend that you do regardless of your product or services.

When it comes to the age range of YouTube users, YouTube reaches 83-93% of the population between the ages of 18 to 64 years old. It drops off a bit to 60% of the population ages 65 and older but still, having 60% of the population using your platform regularly is absolutely incredible. Now think about that 83-93% statistic! YouTube reaches between 83-93% of the population 64 years old and younger! That's a HUGE demographic to reach regularly!

Now let's move on to gender! Again, YouTube rules! YouTube reaches both males and females equally and it reaches A LOT of them! 82% of the male population and 83% of the female population are YouTube users!

As for location of the YouTube user base, the United States has the most users at 239 million, which is beat only by India with 462 million, again, larger population, larger user base. YouTube users in Western Europe come in 3rd with 162.6 million. Other countries like Brazil and Indonesia are not far behind when it comes to its population who are YouTube users. This is a really good spread of demographics for world regions, which means if your business or brand are on YouTube, it will be seen by many people from many different countries. More eyes seeing your business or brand's products and services means more potential profits.

When it comes to education level, again, YouTube rocks with its fairly evenly distributed education levels among its users. 74% of the population with a high school education or less, use YouTube. 85% of the population with at least some college education are YouTube users and 89% of the population with college degrees and higher are YouTube users. This means that your business or brand's products or services are being seen by a majority of the population regardless of education level. All levels are heavily represented here.

And then financial status for YouTube users is incredible! If you want to put your business or brand's products or services in front of as many people as possible that can afford to purchase them, this is THE platform for doing that. **89% of the population that makes OVER $100,000 annually are YouTube users!!** 86% of the population that makes $70,000-$99,999 use YouTube and 83% of the population who make between $30,000-$69,999 also use YouTube. That's a lot of people with a lot of money potentially looking for your products and services!

When it comes to race and ethnicity, you will be reaching 81-93% of all people of different racial and ethnic backgrounds.

YouTube reaches slightly more of the population in urban and suburban area than rural areas but, again, all areas are fairly evenly reached. 85% of the population who live in either urban or suburban areas are YouTube users and 77% of the rural population also use YouTube. So, there's a slight drop off of users when it comes to those who live rurally but it's really negligible in my opinion. YouTube offers access to a great majority of the population in all areas of the population.

Political affiliation is no different than the other demographics. 82% of the population who considers themselves Republican or Republican Leaning are YouTube users and 84% of the population who consider themselves Democrats or Democratic Leaning are YouTube users. Regardless of who you want to market to YouTube has got you covered.

YouTube wasn't always the powerhouse it is today however; more and more people today prefer to watch videos than read an article. We've become a population of avid TV watchers and the demographics are reflecting that clearly. My advice to any of my social media clients would be to make YouTube one of the top 3 social media platforms your business or brand uses to reach potential clients or customers in order to go from likes to profits quickly

CHAPTER 9

SNAPCHAT

"If people believe they share values with a company, they will stay loyal to the brand."

-Howard Schultz

DEMOGRAPHICS:

- **Active Users:** 500 million active monthly users. It is the 6th largest social media platform in the world.[xviii]
- **Age:**
    - 65% of people aged 18-29 use Snapchat
    - 30% of people aged 30-49 use Snapchat
    - 13% of people aged 50-64 use Snapchat
    - 4% of people aged 65+ use Snapchat
- **Gender:** 21% of men and 32% of women use Snapchat
- **Location:**[xix]
    - **India** – 200.97 million users
    - **United States** – 106.24 million users
    - **Pakistan** – 30.21 million users
    - **France** – 27.35 million users
    - **United Kingdom** – 23.67 million users

- **Education Level:**
  - 26% of people with a high school level education or less use Snapchat.
  - 32% of people with some education at the college level use Snapchat.
  - 23% of people with an education beyond the college level, meaning they have graduate or terminal degrees, use Snapchat.
- **Financial Status:**
  - 27% of people who earn less than $30,000 use Snapchat
  - 30% of people who earn between $30,000 to $69,999 use Snapchat
  - 26% of people who earn between $70,000 to $99,999 use Snapchat
  - 25% of people who earn $100,000+ use Snapchat
- **Race & Ethnicity:**
  - 25% of people who are White use Snapchat.
  - 25% of people who are Black use Snapchat.
  - 35% of people who are Hispanic use Snapchat.
  - 25% of people who are English-speaking use Snapchat.
- **Community:**
  - 29% of people who live in an urban area use Snapchat.

- 26% of people who live in a suburban area use Snapchat.
- 27% of people who live in a rural area use Snapchat.

❖ **Political Affiliation:**
- 27% of people who are Republican or Lean Republican use Snapchat.
- 28% of people who are Democrat or Lean Democrat use Snapchat.

What this all tells us:

Know I'll be honest, I've never used Snapchat though I know a lot of people really like it. With 500 million active monthly users, it's the 6th largest social media platform in the world. The essential function of Snapchat is its users can take a picture or video and then add filters, lenses, or other effects and then they can share it with friends. I don't really know how effective Snapchat would be for business marketing personally but according to Social Champ, Snapchat can be a powerful tool for promoting your business and engaging with your audience on a personal level. They suggest offering exclusive discounts and other discounts on Snapchat to get followers and increase your business or brand's reach.

As far as the demographics go, Snapchat is by far a young person's social media platform with the majority of the population's 18–29-year-olds being their main user profile.

From there, it's a huge age drop off as far as their users go with only 30% of the population's 30–49-year-olds using the platform, 13% of the population's 50–64-year-olds and 4% of people over 65 years old using the platform. So, if your products or services are aimed at people over 50 years old, this is definitely not the platform for you. However, if your products or services cater to those 29 years old and under, you might want to give it a try.

When it comes to gender, a slightly higher majority of females (32%) use Snapchat over males (21%).

The majority of Snapchat's users are from India and the United States, followed in third, fourth, and fifth place by Pakistan, France, and the United Kingdom.

When it comes to education, Snapchat's users are pretty evenly distributed among all educational backgrounds.

Most of Snapchat's users make $69,999 annually or less when it comes to financial status. So, it's not a really wealthy audience but that's to be expected from a social media platform that attracts users 29 years old and under.

Race and ethnicity, community, and political affiliation are all very evenly distributed among Snapchat's user base. So, of those who use Snapchat, you're getting a pretty even mix of demographics amongst the younger audience.

CHAPTER 10

FACEBOOK

"The thing that we are trying to do at Facebook is just help people connect and communicate more efficiently."

– Mark Zuckerberg, Founder/Chairman/CEO of Meta

Facebook (now technically known as Meta) has, by far, taken the lead as **THE** social media platform since its inception in 2004. Since then, it has acquired several other platforms, namely WhatsApp, Instagram, Messenger, and Threads (to compete with X).

Facebook's domination in the social media space is the reason I always recommend every business or brand have a page on its platform. It's where the most eyes are, most of the time, and it's a safe bet for all businesses and brands when it comes to building followers and creating a brand.

DEMOGRAPHICS[xx]:

- ❖ **Active Users:** 2.9 billion monthly active users and is the number 1 largest social media platform in the world.
- ❖ **Age:** Whereas Millennials are, on average, the most popular age group of Facebook users, Facebook is actually one of the **least preferred** platforms **among Millennials and Gen Z**. As you'll see later on, they prefer platforms like TikTok, Snapchat, and YouTube.
    - o 67% of people aged 18-29 use Facebook
    - o 75% of people aged 30-49 use Facebook
    - o 69% of people aged 50-64 use Facebook
    - o 58% of people aged 65+ use Facebook
- ❖ **Gender:** The distribution of male to female is fairly even among Facebook users with a slight flip in numbers depending on whether you're looking at global users or only U.S. users.
    - o **Globally**, 56.8% of users are male and 43.2% are female.
    - o **United States**, 54.7% of users are female and 45.3% are male.
    - o **In the U.S. Population Overall:** 59% of men in the U.S. population and 76% of women in the U.S. population use Facebook.

- ❖ **Location:** As far as countries go, India is the country with the highest number of Facebook users but that's to be expected when you compare their population with other countries. More people, more users! The United States has the second highest number of Facebook users and most of the stats in the following chapters are based on Pew Research[xxi] surveys on U.S. adults conducted from 2012-2023. Demographics from other sources will be cited at the time they are presented.
    - o **India** – 385.65 million users
    - o **United States** – 188.6 million users
    - o **Indonesia** – 136.35 million users
    - o **Brazil** – 111.75 million users
    - o **United Kingdom** – 36.8 million users.

To see the complete list of Facebook users by country see the article by Backlinko here: https://backlinko.com/facebook-users[xxii]

- ❖ **Education Level:** Again, this demographic, like the male to female stats, are fairly even across all education levels.
    - o 63% of people with a high school level education or less use Facebook.
    - o 71% of people with some education at the college level use Facebook.

- 70% of people with an education beyond the college level, meaning they have graduate or terminal degrees, use Facebook.

❖ **Financial Income Status:** Again here, like many of the other demographics, the stats are fairly even when it comes to income status and Facebook use.

- 63% of people who earn less than $30,000 use Facebook
- 70% of people who earn between $30,000 to $69,999 use Facebook
- 74% of people who earn between $70,000 to $99,999 use Facebook
- 68% of people who earn $100,000+ use Facebook

❖ **Race & Ethnicity:**
- 69% of people who are White use Facebook.
- 64% of people who are Black use Facebook.
- 66% of people who are Hispanic use Facebook.
- 67% of people who are English-speaking Asian use Facebook.

❖ **Community:**
- 66% of people who live in an urban area use Facebook.
- 68% of people who live in a suburban area use Facebook.

- o 70% of people who live in a rural area use Facebook.
- ❖ **Political Affiliation:**
  - o 70% of people who are Republican or Lean Republican use Facebook.
  - o 67% of people who are Democrat or Lean Democrat use Facebook.
- ❖ **Additional Info:**
  - o 77% of women versus 61% of men use Facebook on both desktop or mobile devices.

What this data tells us:

Of all the social media platforms, Facebook is that one that is the most evenly distributed among all demographics. Meaning, it touches pretty much on every different population your business might want to reach, which is why I tell every client that they need a Facebook page. It is the perfect place to start when beginning to choose which social media platforms you want to be on.

Facebook has 2.9 BILLION monthly active users and is the NUMBER ONE LARGEST social media platform in the world! Again, another reason that I recommend every client have a Facebook Page. It's a huge pool of the population that uses this platform and you would be making a mistake not to have your business or brand be a part of the party.

As far as age goes, many like to say that Facebook is for old people but just look at the demographics. It's not really true. All age groups are pretty fairly represented on Facebook. I think the idea of Facebook being for old people comes from the fact that in the beginning, when Facebook first started, most of the people that used it were college age or younger. Considering that Facebook was founded by two college students for their college peers, that makes total sense. However, as Facebook grew and eventually went public, it opened the platform to all demographics and now people of all ages find Facebook to be a regular part of their daily lives, just like having a cup of coffee in the morning.

When it comes to the gender of those on Facebook, again the it is fairly evenly distributed between male and female users. So, it's a great place to be in order to reach all genders.

Now when it comes to the location of users, if you want to reach people in India or the United States, hands down, Facebook is the best place to be. Again, when you look at the location of demographics it may look like Facebook is an awful place to reach the U.K. population with only 36.8 million users. However, if you consider that the current (2024) population of the U.K. is 67.9 million people, that's INCREDIBLE! Why? Because Facebook reaches more than half of the current U.K. population!

So, it's important when looking at these statistics for all the platforms that you consider the populations of each of these countries. Sometimes it may look like a platform is not reaching that many people but when you factor in the entire population of a certain country you may find out that the platform is performing great there.

When it comes to education level, again, Facebook reaches all educational levels pretty evenly. It reaches slightly more people with a high school or lower education but the numbers are statistically irrelevant in my opinion. You'll pretty much reach all levels of education when you're on Facebook.

Again, when trying to reach people of all financial income levels, you can't do better than Facebook. It reaches pretty much everyone. Are you seeing a trend here? Are you starting to understand why I ALWAYS recommend every client of mine to have a Facebook Page for their business, brand, or non-profit?

The same holds true for users' Race and Ethnicity, Communities, and Political Affiliations. Facebook is evenly distributed amongst ALL of these demographics. It's almost exactly the same percentages for these three specific demographics. This makes Facebook the ideal place to start when choosing your business or brand's first social media platform. Facebook is a great place for individuals and B2B marketers to engage and connect with their target audience

CHAPTER 11

KEEP IT SIMPLE AND HAVE FUN

"The key is to set realistic expectations, then exceed them, preferably in unexpected and helpful ways."

-Richard Branson

Let's face it, with all the different social media platforms out there and all the new ones popping up almost daily (ok, maybe a slight exaggeration), it's easy to get sucked into the excitement and feel like you have to join every single one of them. I mean, more is better, right? Well, no, it's not.

The point of this book is to help you define which social media platforms will give you more bang for your buck, quite literally. Initially you just need to start slowly. Pick 2-3 social media platforms that most closely fit the demographics of your ideal clients or customers. Build your followers up on those platforms first and then as you get more experienced and learn more about your followers you can add a few more platforms if you want. Now I do have a few rules when it comes to building your following on social media.

First, don't skimp on quality. Practically everything you need to build your ideal following on social media can be found for no or low-cost. However, if after searching for an app or service to help with building your email list and following on social media, you can't find any that satisfy your business's needs then you should find one that will serve your needs even if it has a minimal cost.

My point here is to be smart with your business's budget. It's very easy to get pulled into paying for services even if you really don't need them or aren't really ready for them. Running a business or brand requires more effort and money than most people are aware of. Don't waste time and money on items that aren't really necessary but don't use something that is of poor quality either just to keep costs down. Use your common sense to know when it's the right time to purchase something and when a no or low-cost option is good enough.

Second, don't be lazy! Knowing who your ideal client or customer is will take some effort and time to figure out. So, will choosing the best social media platforms to reach those ideal clients or customers. I've seen many people in businesses large and small throw money at things in the hopes that it will save them from having to do the work. They have the mistaken belief that money solves every challenge and that the more money they toss at the problem the easier the situation will become. This is not at all true. In reality, it can actually lead to more problems, the biggest one being financial challenges.

While it is true that if one is blessed with an unlimited budget, it can make solving challenges a little easier but it rarely, if ever, solves them without any effort on your part. Even if you decide to hire someone to take care of your business or brand's social media presence, don't think you're off the hook.

That person you hire is going to need some direction and feedback from you on what the organization's goals are, how you would ideally like those goals to be accomplished, and who your business or brand's ideal clients or customers are. You will ultimately be the one responsible for the brand image that is being put out there for the entire world to see.

Contrary to popular belief, ignorance is not bliss. Ignorance can be death to an organization whose leaders are not in control and taking responsibility for the content, products, services, and campaigns that are being produced. So, you need to always check in with your social media people to find out what they're doing, check out what content is being produced, and make sure it's in direct alignment with your business or brand's objectives. If it's not, you need to give your employee or social media manager some direction and ground rules to follow in order to achieve your business or brand's goals.

Third, don't get things that you don't need. It can be tempting once you get into the social media world, with the technology that's available, to want everything that's out there. I know. I've been there and still sometimes I have to reign myself in. However, getting everything that's available to you can cause great stress and confusion because after a while it becomes impossible to keep track of and ultimately, things start to fall out of view and off the regularly scheduled rotation.

It will also create undue mental stress on you as well because you when have all those things going on, somewhere in the back of your mind, whether it be conscious or not, you will be thinking about all the things you 'have to do'. This can lead to what I call 'overwhelm induced paralysis', which is when your to do list is so long that you become frozen not knowing what to do first.

This is usually when you'll find yourself finding other 'more important' things to do like eating…again…or suddenly deciding that you need to organize the office or go grocery shopping or any number of other distractions. I know some of you are smiling at this because I am sure some of you can identify with this phenomenon. I know I do.

Fourth, keep it simple! Start simply with the basics and add other social media platforms and services as you feel they become necessary for your business or brand. In the beginning, I recommend just having those 3 Must-Haves that I describe in Chapter 2. Those are:

1. A simple business website.
2. A blog.
3. A Facebook business page.

Once you have those three things set up and functioning well. Then you can add 1-2 more social media platforms, in addition to the Facebook business page, once you're sure you're 100% clear on who your ideal clients or customers are, also known as your business avatar. Ideally, you should know this **BEFORE** you even start your business. If you're at all unclear on who that is for you, you **MUST** work on finding out who your ideal audience is.

Not knowing who your ideal clients or customers are before choosing your ideal social media platforms is not only wasting your time but it's also throwing your profits away. You can have the best products and services in the world but if you're not where your ideal clients or customers are, no one will know or care what you have to offer.

Commit to spending an hour or two a week planning what you want to talk about on your business or brand's social media pages in the coming week. During this time, you'll not only decide what the week's theme or promotion is but you'll also create related posts for X (if using), short posts for Facebook, and longer blogs that will post to all of your social media pages from your website. You can also scout online news for relevant articles and studies that will support your theme, brand, products or services.

Once you've gathered and written everything for the week, you can simply preschedule all of it using a social media scheduler like Buffer, Loomly, Later, Hootsuite, or one of the other platforms available. This way you can forget all about it for the rest of the week. Once it's all scheduled it will happen automatically without any extra effort from you. Of course, if you're an overachiever, you can take an entire weekend to plan and create the whole month's social media content too.

After that is all done, it's a good idea to pop on and monitor your social media sites from time to time throughout the week in order to make sure everything is going according to schedule. During this time, you will also respond to any questions or comments your followers may have for you, which helps to build your community and create rapport. Keeping this venue of one-to-one communication open with your followers and supporters will make them feel like they're part of a community or group, which in return will keep them coming back for more. Once you develop a community like this, they will freely share your content, products, and/or services with their friends, family, and co-workers and it becomes a viral referral system!

I know this all sounds like a LOT but I assure you that it's not that hard once you put a system in place and follow it. I also know that I've mentioned a lot of things like social media delivery platforms, creating content for your social media, and creating dialogues with your followers that I haven't explained in this book. This book was created to start you on the road to not only finding your ideal customers or clients but also to teach you how to choose the most profitable social media platforms for your brand. Your business or brand's most profitable social media platforms are the ones where those ideal customers or clients are hanging out.

In my next two books, available later this year, I will go into more detail about how to create the most profitable content for your brand or business that will attract your ideal clients and customers. I will also go into the best ways to promote your social media presence in order to raise awareness of your business or brand as well as attract the ideal customers or clients to it.

FINAL WORDS

"Profit in business comes from repeat customers, customers that boast about your project or service, and that bring friends with them."

– W. Edwards Deming

One of the biggest reasons that I wrote this book in the first place was to help those of you who find social media platforms frustrating and overwhelming. With so many social media platforms out there and new ones popping up practically daily, it's easy to get caught up in the hype and minutia. It's also easy to find yourself swimming in a sea of confusion about which social media platforms are best and most profitable for your business or brand. I wanted to provide a reference to help you distinguish between them all and give you a way to understand each platform's demographics.

Once you know a platform's target audience and you've done the work to figure out your business or brand's ideal customer or client then it's easy to choose which platforms are a match. Doing the work to figure these two things out can mean the difference between social media success and social media distress. It also can be the difference between a business or brand that doesn't do well and one that gets more than likes. It's your brand's path from likes to profits!

Always remember **KNOWLEDGE is POWER** and this book is the first step towards that power. It's about creating a more profitable business or brand. The quote at the beginning of this chapter from W. Edwards Deming is true but if you are on the wrong social media platforms and talking to people who aren't your ideal customers or clients, then you're not likely to find your path to profits there. Don't get me wrong, you're likely to find a client or customer or two but you're unlikely to get any repeat customers. Why? Because if your business or brand is on the wrong platform, you're speaking to the wrong audience. You're speaking to people who don't need or want what your brand has to offer. The platform must match your brand's ideal avatar or as close to those demographics as possible. You will most likely not find an exact match but you can find the BEST match available and that can make all the difference.

This book is not about showing you specifically which social media platform is the best fit for your business or brand. It's about showing you how to find the information you need to make the best decision for your business or brand. It's about showing you how to analyze that information. It's about showing you how to figure out your business or brand's ideal avatar (a.k.a. ideal customer or client). Once those things are accomplished, it's about choosing the social media platforms that are the best match for your ideal avatar. Remember, you could have the best products or services in the world with the best marketing messages available, written by the best marketers in the world but if you are marketing on the wrong social media platform, you are talking to the wrong audience! The wrong audience equals poor or no profits!

I am sure you have noticed that this book hasn't covered every social media platform out there. That would be impossible to do in one book…or even ten books for that matter. There are too many social media platforms to mention and more popping up daily. It would be an impossible task for anyone. I have also purposely left some social media platforms out that many would say are essential or popular. TikTok being one of them.

TikTok as of late has had some BIG issues as far as security and various other challenges. I have left it off the list for several reasons. The first being that I do not use TikTok. I never have used it and I don't see a future in which I ever will use it. That does not mean that you can't use it. Just use the resources I've taught you about in this book to analyze the platform and compare it to your business or brand's ideal avatar. If it's a fit and you feel it's one that you want to use, then use it. I will also advise you to research the security issues involved with using that platform before you dive in. I would also advise you to see if TikTok's platform is even available to use in your country. Many countries have banned the use of TikTok due to security and political issues. So do your due diligence before deciding to use that platform.

I also haven't mentioned messaging apps like Facebook's Messenger, WhatsApp, Telegram, Discord, and others that have slowly become avenues for businesses and brands to communicate with their ideal customers or clients. Maybe in a future book I'll cover these apps and their uses but it would be too much for a book of this length. They are used somewhat differently from other social media platforms so it just didn't feel like a good fit for this book. However, figuring out if those apps are a fit for your business or brand would follow the same guidelines and steps that were used for those social media platforms covered in this book.

Demographics are constantly changing. They are kind of a living thing, ebbing and flowing with the population, the economy, the world situation, and more. As an example, the number of social media users worldwide has increased by 320 million people from January 2023 to January 2024. That's a lot of change! Those 320 million people bring with them different demographics as well. 320 million people can change a social media platform's user base demographics in an instant. That's why it's next to impossible to do these exercises once and be done. Social media use, just like any other aspect of a business or brand, needs to reviewed and updated frequently in order to keep up with the trends. I would recommend that, at a minimum, you review not only your ideal customers or clients but also the social media platforms your business or brands use once a year. Every six months would be ideal. Just make it part of your yearly or bi-yearly business review. It should only take a few hours at most once or twice a year to accomplish and it will ensure that your business or brand stays on the path from likes to profits!

Now, I realize that not every person has the desire, inclination, or skills needed to BE the social media manager for their business or brand. If you identify with that statement have no fear. It doesn't mean all is hopeless and your business or brand has to do without a social media presence. All it means is that you have to ask for some help.

There are many ways for your business or brand to get help with its social media marketing. There are many people and organizations out there that excel at not only researching the best social media platforms for a business or brand but they also excel at setting up social media pages and accounts, creating content, and interacting with social media followers. If you are looking for someone to do these tasks for you, there are several places to look to get started with your search. Many of these options are low cost so that's always a plus, right?

Your Circle of Family and Friends

The first place you can look for someone to help you with your social media marketing is in your own circle of family and friends. Just because you might not be inclined to figure out all this social media stuff doesn't mean someone close to you can't do it for you. It is very likely that someone you know intimately like a family member or close friend knows the ins and outs of social media like it's their native language. Social media has become such a daily ritual for so many people that finding someone in your intimate circle of influence to help you is most likely an easy ask. It's my bet that they would love to be a part of your business or brand's growth and help you on your journey from likes to profits.

Most people who are the techie sort look for reasons to play around with it all, so my guess is if you approach someone in your circle who meets those criteria, they will most likely jump at the chance to show off their skills to you. Many times, when you ask someone in your friends or family circle to help you, they won't ask for compensation of any kind in return. However, you are asking them to help your business or brand out, so be fair. Just because they are a friend or family member doesn't mean they should be considered free labor. You should always insist on some kind of payment for their time and labor.

Teenagers or College Students

Now if no one in your family or friends circle has the time or skills to help you out, you can move to the next possibility – computer/social media savvy teenagers or college students.

Most teenagers and college students are experts when it comes to computers and social media because they grew up with it. They have known nothing else. It's part of their daily routine.

According to a 2022 Pew Research survey[xxiii] "more than half of teens say it would be difficult for them to give up social media." Another Pew Research survey found that 1 in 5 teens state that they are on YouTube or TikTok "almost constantly" and 9 in 10 teens say they use the internet at least daily. A 2018 Common Sense Media report show that 70% of teens log in to social media multiple times a day, and 16% check it almost constantly. Another Common Sense Media report[xxiv] showed that 13 year-olds check their social media accounts and texts a MINIMUM of 100 times a day and spend NINE HOURS A DAY on social media! That nine hours is more than the time they spend sleeping or being with their parents and it doesn't include time on social media at school or doing homework!

So, I think you know where I am going here. Teens and college students are EXPERTS at social media! That's why this group is a virtual goldmine of knowledge and information on the subject. They grew up with computers and social media. To them, it's a fact of life and something that everyone should innately know how to use. It's because of this mindset that they are the second group I recommend going to if you're looking for a low-cost solution for your social media management.

Now the really great thing about asking teenagers or college students for help with your social media is that you might actually have one or two of them in your house. However, if you don't have one of your very own, most high school or college front desks can tell you if they have a computer club with students that can help you with your social media for extra course credit or even as a side job. Most likely you will be directed towards one or two young social media masters who would love to show off their techie skills and make a little money.

Customer or Supporter Base

Another great place to find someone to help you with your business or brand's social media marketing is within your customer or client base. Just announce to your customers or clients that you need a volunteer to help your business or brand develop and maintain its social media presence. There are many people who would love the chance to help their favorite business or brand be more successful. Sometimes you just have to ask.

This an especially great tactic if you are a non-profit. As a non-profit, there is usually very little budget for a social media manager. However, there are many people out there who would love to contribute to your mission but they can't afford to do so financially. Volunteering is a great way for them to help your non-profit with its cause and mission without placing financial difficulties on themselves. Pulling from a volunteer base allows you and your organization access a wide variety of talents that it might not have access to otherwise.

Also, volunteers are an exceptional group of people with amazing hearts and because of that you will most likely get someone helping who genuinely cares about your organization's success. One or two passionate volunteers who are in alignment with your organization's mission and goals can make such a huge difference in the type of followers and supporters that you will start getting as well. It will also create a community around your business, brand, or non-profit. When this happens it can cause a huge uptick of new customers, clients, or donors to find your business, brand, or non-profit because everyone wants to be a part of an organization that makes them feel like they belong. Social media communities help people feel like they are a part of something that's bigger than themselves as well.

Job Websites

If you look in the previous three areas and are still having challenges trying to find the right person to help you with your social media marketing, don't panic.

Sites like Upwork, Fiverr, and Freelancer offer a variety of freelance social media managers. These sites are filled with freelancers and digital nomads who generally work for themselves by taking projects like this from people like you. Many of these sites you can either post that you are looking for someone to help you set up and manage the social media for your business or brand and wait for someone to contact you. Conversely, many of these sites show you a list of people who do social media management and you can choose someone that fits your budget and needs.

Another place to find freelancers or independent contractors is on niche job boards like Acadium, Facebook, Twitter, Instagram, Guru, Hubstaff Talent, People Per Hour, Simply Hired, LinkedIn and more.

I have used some of these sites for various services I've needed for my business including for hiring the graphic designer for my previous books, *Making Your Business A Social Media Superstar: The Step-by-Step Guide to Creating, Maintaining, and Promoting Your Online Presence* and *The Massage Disadvantage*. You can get amazing quality work inexpensively.

Prices on Fiverr.com start at $5 per job – thus the name – and usually have many add-ons that are needed in order to do the whole job well but generally speaking it's really easy to get great help there inexpensively.

Independent Contractors or Social Media Companies

If you're looking for a more professional solution to your social media management needs then I would suggest hiring a freelancer or independent contractor that does social media management as a profession. Some of them even started on sites like Fiverr.com and then when they built up their skill and reputation, they moved on to being their own boss and creating their own freelance company.

Many freelancers or independent contractors started like me, which is friends and family came to me asking for help with their social media and eventually word got around and I started my own freelance business doing social media management and that eventually led to clients asking me to build their websites and other types of freelance work. Now most people find me by word of mouth but I do have a website with all my services listed as well as my portfolio.

Freelancers or independent contractors generally charge more than people you will find on sites like Fiverr.com but they sometimes have a little more freedom when it comes to pricing than a social media or digital agency. That being said, most freelancers and independent contractors have to pay for their own 'benefits' like health and dental insurance, etcetera, so don't expect them to always give you a bargain. Most cannot do that due to the fact that they, too, have a need to eat and have shelter. I say this because many times people have thought that because I was a freelance social media manager, I should do my job for next to nothing. Be kind to your freelance and independent contractor friends and acquaintances. Most are professionals with a proven track record and you are getting them cheap in comparison to what a social media or digital agency would charge you for the same services.

When it comes to social media or digital agencies, you will get trained professionals but they can be quite expensive and many times you don't get the close personal attention that you usually get from a freelancer or independent contractor.

Agencies tend to load their social media managers down with clients and that really doesn't leave a lot of time or room for the social media manager to give you the personal attention your business or brand needs. I know this for a fact because I worked for a digital agency for several years. I initially started off with 10 clients that were my responsibility. After about 6 months, the other social media manager left the agency and I was tasked with her 10 clients. Soon after that, the only other part time social media manager that the agency had besides me, was given a different position in the agency and I got all her clients as well. In the end, I had 25+ clients that I was responsible for on a daily basis. I wasn't able to give each one the attention that I would have liked to give them, so I eventually decided to leave the agency and become a freelance social media manager. So, I am very sympathetic to freelancers, being one myself.

As I've said, social media or digital agencies can be quite expensive so if you're thinking of going with that option, I would advise that to be your last choice after you've tried all other options first. Just my opinion, of course, but it's my book, so I'm allowed.

Your best bet in my opinion, should you decide that hiring someone to handle your social media is your best option, would be to hire a freelancer or independent contractor. Freelancers and independent contractors are people who work for themselves and can be hired on a job-to-job basis. Many are open to being hired long-term. They are not an employee of your business or brand but rather a business that you hire to do certain jobs. I've been a freelancer/independent contractor for various motivational speakers, corporations, non-profits, and individuals for almost two decades now. Many of them I have worked for long-term. I have worked for Tony Robbins' companies for almost that entire two decades but I am not an employee of his company. I am an independent contractor, which means I am not obligated to take a job if I don't want to.

However, independent contractors and freelancers generally like to have clients who stay with them long-term so most will happily sign up to help you with a project that has no specific end to it. Generally, you would agree to either a per hour, per project, or per month rate of pay and you will pay the contractor for the jobs that they do on a regular basis. Always remember that independent contractors and freelancers work for themselves and they have regular bills to pay just like you do, so make sure that you do the right thing when it comes to paying them.

Now there are several places online where you can find and hire independent contractors and freelancers. Fiverr.com is one of them. It's possible to find someone on there that you like and who may want to stay on with you after they do a few jobs for you. It never hurts to ask. Many people on Fiverr.com and other sites are looking for more steady, regular work and would welcome an offer to do regular work for you.

For example, the freelancer that I hired to make the book cover for my previous two books was listed on Fiverr.com. I hired him to do the book cover for the first book that I cowrote and I liked working with him. So, when I wrote my first solo book, I contacted him again and he was thrilled to work with me again and we have stayed in touch since. He now has his own company and website and is doing really well. Many freelancers and independent contractors start their businesses by finding clients on freelance sites like Fiverr and others.

Other sites that I recommend would be Freelancer.com, LinkedIn, Upwork, Remote, Guru, PeoplePerHour, and 99designs and those are just a few.

Remember, Everything Takes Time…

Everything takes time and despite what we might have been sold on when computers came on the scene…everything still takes time…and usually more time than we think it should. Learning who your ideal clients or customers are and then analyzing and choosing the most profitable social media platforms for your brand is no different.

Improvement takes time. I know for some this can be frustrating. We've turned into a society that loves and wants instant rewards but the best things do indeed take time. Relish in the journey. Enjoy every step towards improving your business and its profits. Think of how proud you will be when you've taken the steps necessary to create a more profitable business or brand. You've got this!

FREE GIFTS JUST FOR YOU!

I also want to take this time to remind you about the FREE GIFTS I've created just for my readers. I created this FREE content to help you and your business or brand advance "From Likes to Profits". Here is what is included:

- **2024 Easy Reference Social Media Demographics Chart** – A great reference to remind you of the different social media platforms and their specific demographics.
- **Discovering Your Ideal Customers or Clients Worksheet** – Gain clarity on your ideal customer avatar by analyzing demographics, interests, and identifying common traits.
- **Top 10 Things to Consider BEFORE Hiring a Social Media Manager** – Evaluate your business needs and objectives to determine the specific skills and expertise required from a social media manager.

GET YOUR FREE GIFTS NOW BY GOING TO:
https://goldspielcreativeenterprises.com/free-gifts-from-likes-to-profits/

CONNECT WITH ME ON FACEBOOK!
Join my *Small Business Wealth Marketing* private Facebook community here:
https://www.facebook.com/groups/smallbusinesswealthmarketing/

PLEASE DO ME A HUGE FAVOR

Please do me a huge favor, if you have been inspired by my books and want to help others get inspired too, here are some action steps you can take immediately to make a positive difference:

Write a review on Amazon for this book. Reviews are critical for authors, helping us sell more books and deliver more value to our readers. It also helps people looking for my books, find them more easily. People are more apt to buy a book like this if there are positive reviews telling them how the book has helped its readers personally.

Gift my books. Gift my books to friends, family, colleagues and even strangers so that they can also learn from them.

Share your thoughts. Please share your thoughts about this book on X, Facebook, Instagram, LinkedIn, or any other of your favorite social media platforms or write a book review and share it. It helps other people find my books.

Amazon Author Page:
https://www.amazon.com/stores/Veronica-Goldspiel/author/B0D466HRG9

Thank you! I can't wait to hear how this book has helped you to achieve your social media goals. Please write to me and let me know all about your successes! I look forward to hearing from you. You can contact me at Veronica@GoldspielCreativeEnterprises.com.

ABOUT THE AUTHOR

Photo Credit: Dr. Alan Goldspiel

Veronica Goldspiel, a veteran freelancer with over two decades of experience, has worked with top motivational and self-improvement speakers worldwide, including luminaries like Tony Robbins and T. Harv Eker.

Veronica's expertise spans various sectors, from healthcare to entertainment and offers a holistic approach to business and personal growth. Her extensive skills in social media management, content creation, and book publishing as well as health and wellness continue to empower clients globally.

As an author, Veronica penned works such as *Making Your Business a Social Media Superstar: A Step-by-Step Guide to Creating, Maintaining, and Promoting Your Online Presence*, and co-authored *The Massage Disadvantage*. Her commitment to sharing knowledge extends beyond books, as she regularly contributes to platforms like www.thefreelancerslife.com.

Driven by a passion to empower others, Veronica focuses on producing books across her many areas of expertise to aid individuals in overcoming their challenges and to more easily achieve their aspirations. When she's not immersed in writing, Veronica can be found honing her barista skills with her espresso machine, engrossed in a good read, or enjoying beach outings with her husband, Alan.

You can connect with Veronica at: www.goldspielcreativeenterprises.com to turn your business or brand's "likes into profits."

OTHER BOOKS BY AUTHOR

Making Your Business a Social Media Superstar: The Step-by-Step Guide to Creating, Maintaining, and Promoting Your Online Presence (as Veronica Buhl)

The Massage Disadvantage (Co-author as Veronica Buhl)

[i] Worldwide Daily Social Media Usage (New 2024 Data) (November 28, 2023) Primary Reasons for Using Social Media – Exploding Topics - https://explodingtopics.com/blog/social-media-usage
[ii] Instagram by the Numbers: Stats, Demographics, and Fun Facts (February 20, 2024) - Omnicore - https://www.omnicoreagency.com/instagram-statistics
[iii] 50+ Must-Know Social Media Marketing Statistics for 2024 (February 8, 2024) – Sprout Social - https://sproutsocial.com/insights/social-media-statistics/
[iv] Which Social Media Platforms are Most Popular (January 31, 2024) – Pew Research Center - https://www.pewresearch.org/internet/fact-sheet/social-media
[v] X Shares New Insights Into Platform Usage and Engagement – Social Media Today (March 18, 2024) - https://www.socialmediatoday.com/news/x-formerly-twitter-shares-insights-platform-usage-engagement/710641/
[vi] X (Formerly Twitter) User Age, Gender, and Demographic Stats (2024) (November 20, 2023) – Exploding Topics https://explodingtopics.com/blog/x-user-stats#region
[vii] X (Formerly Twitter) User Age, Gender, and Demographic Stats (2024) (November 20, 2023) – Exploding Topics https://explodingtopics.com/blog/x-user-stats#region
[viii] 11 Best Social Media Platforms of 2024 (January 17, 2024) – Khoros - https://khoros.com/blog/11-best-social-media-platforms-of-2024
[ix] Instagram Statistics: Key Demographic and User Numbers (March 25, 2024) – Backlinko - https://backlinko.com/instagram-users
[x] Instagram Statistics: Key Demographic and User Numbers (March 25, 2024) – Backlinko - https://backlinko.com/instagram-users
[xi] Marketing to Moms as a Consumer Group (March 8, 2023) – Forbes - https://www.forbes.com/sites/forbesagencycouncil/2023/03/08/marketing-to-moms-as-a-consumer-group
[xii] Your Audience is Here. And They're Ready to Shop – Pinterest Business - https://business.pinterest.com/audience
[xiii] Pinterest Revenue and Usage Statistics (2024) (February 22, 2024) – Business of Apps - https://www.businessofapps.com/data/pinterest-statistics
[xiv] 51 LinkedIn Statistics You Need to Know in 2024 (February 15, 2024) – Hootsuite Blog - https://blog.hootsuite.com/linkedin-statistics-business/
[xv] 51 LinkedIn Statistics You Need to Know in 2024 (February 15, 2024) – Hootsuite Blog - https://blog.hootsuite.com/linkedin-statistics-business/

[xvi] YouTube Statistics 2024 (Demographics, Users By Country and More) (April 1, 2024) – Global Media Insight - https://www.globalmediainsight.com/blog/youtube-users-statistics

[xvii] YouTube Statistics 2024 (Demographics, Users By Country and More) (April 1, 2024) – Global Media Insight - https://www.globalmediainsight.com/blog/youtube-users-statistics

[xviii] TikTok User Statistics 2024: Everything You Need To Know (March 7, 2024) – Search Logistics - https://www.searchlogistics.com/learn/statistics/tiktok-user-statistics

[xix] Leading Countries Based on Snapchat Audience Size as of January 2024 – Statista - https://www.statista.com/statistics/315405/snapchat-user-region-distribution/

[xx] Social Media Fact Sheet (January 31, 2024) – Pew Research Center - https://www.pewresearch.org/internet/fact-sheet/social-media

[xxi] Social Media Fact Sheet (January 31, 2024) – Pew Research Center - https://www.pewresearch.org/internet/fact-sheet/social-media/

[xxii] Facebook User and Growth Statistics - Facebook Users by Country (February 23, 2024) – Backlinko - https://backlinko.com/facebook-users

[xxiii] Teens and Social Media: Key Findings from Pew Research Center Surveys (April 24, 2023) – Pew Research Center - https://www.pewresearch.org/short-reads/2023/04/24/teens-and-social-media-key-findings-from-pew-research-center-surveys/

[xxiv] Teens Use an Average of Nine Hours of Media Per Day While Tweens Use Six Hours – Stomp Out Bulling (2024) - https://www.stompoutbullying.org/blog/teens-use-average-nine-hours-media-day-while-tweens-use-six-hours

www.ingramcontent.com/pod-product-compliance
Lightning Source LLC
LaVergne TN
LVHW051840080426
835512LV00018B/2989